NICOLAS DARVAS

HOW I MADE $ 2,000,000 IN THE STOCK MARKET

SANAGE
PUBLISHING HOUSE

Paperback: 978-939574139-2

Printed by:

Sanage Publishing House LLP
Mumbai, India

sanagepublishing@gmail.com

Nicolas Darvas was a dancer, self-taught investor and author. He is best known for his book, "How I Made $2,000,000 in the Stock Market." He discovered investing in 1952, when a Toronto nightclub, unable to pay him in cash, instead paid him with shares. It was on a two-year tour of the world that he initially developed his 'Darvas Box' method of screening stocks - a method of picking stocks based on the stock's price and volume - and later went on to refine this to remove any human element from his trading to susbtantial success.

Nicolas Darvas is regarded as one of the best traders in the history of the market and his method, whilst complicated and difficult to master, has been rigorously tested and has been found to be one of the best trading systems yet developed.

TABLE OF CONTENTS

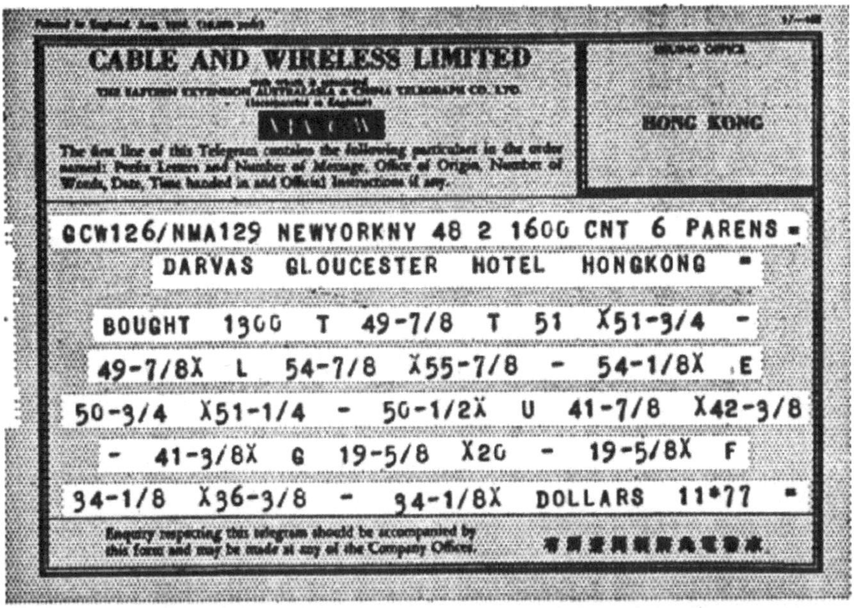

CABLE AND WIRELESS LIMITED

HONG KONG

GCW126/NMA129 NEWYORKNY 48 2 1600 CNT 6 PARENS =
DARVAS GLOUCESTER HOTEL HONGKONG =
BOUGHT 1300 T 49-7/8 T 51 X51-3/4 -
49-7/8X L 54-7/8 X55-7/8 - 54-1/8X E
50-3/4 X51-1/4 - 50-1/2X U 41-7/8 X42-3/8
- 41-3/8X G 19-5/8 X20 - 19-5/8X F
34-1/8 X36-3/8 - 34-1/8X DOLLARS 11*77 =

Enquiry respecting this telegram should be accompanied by this form and may be made at any of the Company Offices.

In the morning of September 3, 1958, the following cable arrived at the

Gloucester Hotel in the Crown Colony of Hong Kong:

"BOUGHT 1300 THIOKOL 49⅞ . . ."

This purchase represented one part of a chain of purchases that were to

net $2,000,000 in eighteen months.

And this is the story of the events that led up to it...

THE GAMBLER

CHAPTER 1

CANADIAN PERIOD

It was November 1952. I was playing in Manhattan's "Latin Quarter" in New York when my agent telephoned. He had received an offer for me and my dancing partner, Julia, to appear in a Toronto nightclub. This was owned by twin brothers, Al and Harry Smith, who made me a very unusual proposition. They offered to pay me in stock instead of money. I have had some strange experiences in show business, but this was a new one.

I made further inquiries and found they were prepared to give me 6,000 shares in a company called BRILUND. This was a Canadian mining firm in which they were interested. The stock at that time was quoted at 50 cents a share.

I knew stocks went up and down—that was about all I did know—so I asked the Smith brothers if they would give me the following guarantee: if the stock went below 50 cents, they would make up the difference. They agreed to do this for a period of six months.

It so happened that I could not keep that Toronto date. I felt badly about letting the brothers down, so I offered to buy the stock as a gesture. I sent them a check for $3,000 and received 6,000 shares of BRILUND stock.

I thought no more about it until one day, two months later, I idly glanced at the stock's price in the paper. I shot upright in my chair. My 50-cent BRILUND stock was quoted at $1.90. I sold it at once and made a profit of close to $8,000.

At first I could not believe it. It was like magic to me. I felt like the man who went to the races for the first time and with beginner's luck backed every winner. Cashing his winnings he simply inquired: "How long has this been going on?"

I decided I had been missing a good thing all my life. I made up my mind to go into the stock market. I have never gone back on this decision, but little did I know what problems I would encounter in this unknown jungle.

I knew absolutely nothing about the stock market. I was not even aware, for instance, that there was one in New York. All I had heard about were Canadian stocks, particularly mining shares. As they had been very good to me, obviously the smart thing to do was to stay with them.

But how to start? How to find what stocks to buy? You could not pick them out with a pin. You must have information. That was my major problem: how to obtain it. I now realize that this is, in fact, impossible for the ordinary man, but then I thought I had only to ask enough people to learn the great secret. I thought if I asked often enough I would get acquainted with people in the .know. I asked everybody I met if they had any stock market information. Working in nightclubs I meet rich people. Rich people must know.

So I asked them. The question was always on my lips: *T)o you know a good stock?" Oddly enough, everybody did seem to know one. It was surprising. Apparently I was the only man in America who did not have his own first-hand stock market information. I listened eagerly to what they had to say and religiously followed their tips. Whatever I was told to buy, I bought. It took me a long time to discover that this is one method that never works.

I was the perfect pattern of the optimistic, clueless small operator who plunges repeatedly in and out of the market. I bought stock in companies whose names I could not pronounce. What they did and where they came from, I had no idea. Someone told someone who told me. There could have been no more slaphappy, ignorant buyer than I was. All I knew was what the last headwaiter in the last nightclub I had performed in had told me was good.

Early in 1953 I was performing in Toronto. Because of my first extraordinary $8,000 break with BRILUND, Canada was the land of financial milk and honey as far as I was concerned, so I decided this was a good place to go looking for a "hot tip." I asked several people if they knew a good, reliable broker, and eventually I was recommended to one.

I must admit I was startled and disappointed when I found his office. It was a tiny, dingy, prison-like room full of books, with strange scrawls on the walls. Later I found out that these are called "charts." There did not seem much smell of success or efficiency. Sitting at a rolltop desk was a busy little man poring over statistics and books. When I asked him if he knew a good stock he reacted at once.

He smiled and pulled out of his pocket a dividend check bearing the name of a famous gold company, KERR-ADDISON.

He stood up and said: "My friend, take a good look at that. That dividend check is worth five times what my father paid for the original stock. That is the sort of stock everyone looks for."

A dividend five times the price of the original stock! This excited me as it would any man. The dividend was 80 cents so his father must have paid only 16 cents for the stock. It looked beautiful to me. I did not realize he had probably been holding his father's stock for thirty- five years.

The little man described to me how he had been looking for that kind of stock for years. In view of his father's success he felt the answer must be in gold mines. He confided to me that he had at last found it. It was called EASTERN MALARTIC. Working with his production figures, estimates and financial information, he reckoned that these gold mines were capable of twice their present gold production, therefore five dollars invested in their stock would soon be worth ten dollars.

On this piece of erudite information I immediately bought 1,000 shares of EASTERN MALARTIC at 290 cents. As I watched anxiously, it went to 270 cents, then to 260. Within weeks it was down to 241 cents, and I hastily sold my stock. I decided this painstaking, statistically minded broker did not have the answer to making a fortune.

Yet the whole thing continued to fascinate me. I went on following any tip but I seldom made money. If I did, it was immediately offset by my losses.

I was such a novice that I did not even understand about broker's commission and transfer taxes. For instance, I bought KAYRAND MINES in January 1953. It was a 10-cent stock, and I bought 10,000 shares.

I watched the market like a cat and when next day KAYRAND went to 11 cents per share, I called my broker and told him to sell. By my reckoning I had made $100 in 24 hours, and I thought I was being smart by taking a quick small profit.

When I talked to my broker again he said: "Why did you decide to take a loss?"—"A loss?" I had made a hundred dollars!

He gently explained to me that the broker's commission for buying 10,000 shares was $50, and for reselling the shares next day it was another $50. In addition, there were transfer taxes on the sale. KAYRAND was just one of the many strange stocks I owned at that time. Others included MOGUL MINES, CONSOLIDATED SUD - BURY BASIN MINES, QUEBEC SMELTING, REXSPAR, JAYE EXPLORATION. I made money on none of them.

Yet I spent a happy year on this Canadian buying and selling. I felt I was the successful businessman, the big stock market operator. I jumped in and out of the market like a grasshopper. I was delighted if I made two points. I often owned 25 to 30 stocks at one time, all in small parcels.

For some of them I acquired a special liking. This came about for different reasons. Sometimes it was because they were given to me by a good friend of mine—other times, because I had started by making money with them. This led me to prefer these stocks more than others, and before I knew what I was doing I had started to keep "pets."

I thought of them as something belonging to me, like members of my family. I praised their virtues day and night. I talked about them as one talks about his children. It did not bother me that no one else could see any special virtue in my pet stocks to distinguish them from any other stocks. This state of mind lasted until I realized that my pet stocks were causing me my heaviest losses.

In a few months my record of transactions looked like the trading record of a small-scale stock exchange. I felt I was doing all right. I appeared to be ahead. If I had carefully studied my statements I would not have felt quite so happy. I would have realized that, like a horse player, I was buoyed up and excited by small gains, and overlooked my losses. I completely ignored the fact that I was holding a lot of stock which was standing well below the price I had paid for it and looked like staying there.

It was a period of wild, foolish gambling with no effort to find the reasons for my operations. I followed "hunches." I went by god-sent names, rumors of uranium-finds, oil strikes, anything anyone told me. When there were constant losses an occasional small gain gave me hope, like the carrot before the donkey's nose.

Then one day, after I had been buying and selling for about seven months, I decided to go over my books. When I added up the values of the bad stocks I was holding I found I had lost almost $3,000.

It was on that day that I began to suspect there was something wrong with my moneymaking scheme. A ghost at the back of my mind began to whisper to me that, in fact, I had no idea what I was doing.

Yet I was still ahead. I consoled myself that I had not touched the

$3,000 I had originally paid for BRILUND, and I had about $5,000 of my profit from that transaction besides. But, if I continued like this, how much longer would I keep it?

Here is just one page from my profit-and-loss accounting. It tells the whole sad story of defeat in microcosm.

OLD SMOKY GAS & OILS Bought at 19 cents Sold at 10 cents KAYRAND MINES Bought at 12 cents Sold at 8 cents

REXSPAR Bought at 130 cents Sold at 110 cents

QUEBEC SMELTING & REFINING Bought at 22 cents Sold at 14 cents

Obsessed by my carrot-before-the-nose gains, I had not noticed I was losing an average of a hundred dollars a week.

It was my first stock market dilemma. The market had several much more serious dilemmas in store for me in the next six years but this one was in some ways the worst. On my decision at this point depended whether I would continue to operate in the market.

I decided to stay and have another try.

The next problem was what to do. There must be a different way. Could I improve my approach? It had been proved to me that it was wrong to listen to nightclub customers, headwaiters, stage-hands. They were only amateurs like myself and, however confidently they offered their tips, they did not know any more than I did.

I gazed at page after page of my brokerage statements, which said: Bought 90 cents, sold 82 . . . Bought 65 cents, sold 48...

Who could help me to discover the secrets of the stock market? I had started to read Canadian financial publications as well as Canadian stock tables. I had begun increasingly to glance at advisory newssheets, which gave tips about stocks listed on the Toronto Stock Exchange.

I had already decided that if I were to go on, I would need

professional help, so I subscribed to some advisory services, which gave financial information. After all, I reasoned, these were the experts. I would follow their professional advice and quit buying stock on the odd tip from a stranger or an amateur stock-fancier like myself. If I followed their skilled, sensible teaching, I must succeed.

There were financial advisory services that offered a trial subscription of four copies of their information-sheets for one dollar. You could have these as a goodwill taste before you began seriously to buy their valuable service.

I put down a dozen or so dollars for trial subscriptions and eagerly read the sheets they sent me.

In New York, there are reputable financial services, but the Canadian sheets that I bought were strictly for the sucker trade. How was I to know this? These financial advice sheets delighted and excited me. They made stock market speculation sound so urgent and easy.

They would come out with huge headlines saying:

"Buy this stock now before it is too late! " "Buy to the full extent of your resources!"

"If your broker advises you against it, get rid of your broker!"

"This stock will give you a profit of 100% or more!"

This, of course, seemed like real, red-hot information. This was much more authentic than the odd tip picked up in a restaurant.

I read these promotion sheets eagerly. They were always filled with much unselfishness and brotherly love. One of them said:

"For the first time in the history of Canadian finance the little fellow will have the fantastic opportunity of getting in on the ground floor of a brilliant new development.

"The plutocrats of Wall Street have been trying to acquire all the stock in our company, but in clear defiance of the evil traditions we are only interested in the participation of investors of moderate means. People like you. ... "

But this was me! They understood my position exactly. I was the typical little fellow to be pitied for the way he was pushed around by the Wall Street plutocrats. I should only have been pitied for my stupidity.

I would rush to the telephone to buy the stock they recommended. It invariably went down. I could not understand this but I was not the slightest bit worried. They must know what they were talking about. The next stock must go up. It seldom did.

I did not know it but I was already coming up against one of the great pitfalls of the small operator—the almost insoluble problem of when to enter the market. These sudden drops immediately after he has invested his money are one of the most mystifying phenomena facing the amateur. It took me years to realize that when these financial tipsters advise the small operator to buy a stock, those professionals who have bought the stock much earlier on inside information are selling.

Simultaneously with the withdrawal of the inside-track money, the small sucker money is coming in. They are not firstest with the mostest, but lastest with the leastest. They are far too late, and their money is always too small to support the stock at its false high point once the professionals are out.

I know this now, but at that time I had no idea why stocks behaved like that. I thought it was just bad luck that they dropped after I bought them. When I look back I know that I was all set at this period to lose everything I had.

When I did invest $100 I almost always lost $20 or $30 at once. But a few stocks did go up and I was comparatively happy.

Even when I had to go to New York I continued to telephone my orders to brokers in Toronto.

I did that because I did not even know you could transact Canadian stock exchange business through a New York broker. The Toronto brokers would telephone tips and I always bought the stock they or the Canadian financial advisory services suggested. Like all small hit-and- miss operators, I put down my losses to bad luck. I knew—I was certain—that one day I would have good luck. I was not wrong all the time—in some ways it would have been better if I had been. Once in a while I made a few dollars. It was always a complete accident.

Here is an example. The Canadian stock tables had become obsessive reading with me. One day when I was looking through them I saw a stock called CALDER BOUSQUET. I still do not know what it was or what the company produces. But it was such a pretty name. I liked the sound of it, so I bought 5,000 shares at 18 cents, for a total of $900.

Then I had to fly to Madrid on a dancing engagement. One month later when I came back I opened the paper and looked for the name. It had gone up to 3 6 cents. That was double the price I had paid. I sold it— and made $900. It was just blind luck.

It was doubly blind luck because not only had it gone up for no good reason but if I had not been dancing in Spain I would certainly have sold the stock when it rose to 22 cents. I could not get Canadian stock quotations while I was in Spain so I was saved from selling too soon by being in blissful ignorance concerning the stock's movements.

This was a strange, mad period, but it only seems so in retrospect. At that time I felt I was really beginning to be a big-time operator. I was proud of myself because I was working on tips of a more educated nature than my previous headwaiter, dressing-room information. My Canadian brokers called me, my financial services advised me, and if I did get a tip I felt I was getting it from the source. I cultivated more and more the society of prosperous businessmen in cocktail lounges who told me about oil companies which were going to strike it rich. They whispered where there was uranium in Alaska; they confided about sensational developments in Quebec. All these were guaranteed to make a great fortune in the future if you could only get into the stocks now. I did, but they did not make me any money.

By the end of 1953, when I returned to New York, my $11,000 was down to $5,800. Once again I had to reconsider my position. The businessmen's tips did not produce the Eldorado they promised. The advisory services did not provide the information, which enables you to make money in the stock market. Their stocks tended much more to go down than up. I could not get quotes for some of my

Canadian stocks in the New York newspapers, yet stock quotations fascinated me so much that I began to read the financial columns in papers like The New York Times, the New York Herald Tribune, and The Wall Street Journal. I did not buy any of the stocks that the New York exchanges quoted, but I still remember the impact of the beautiful names of some of the stocks and the appeal of some of the mysterious phrases like "over the counter."

The more I read, the more I became interested in the New York market. I decided to sell all my Canadian stock except for OLD SMOKY GAS & OILS—and I kept this one because the man who gave me the stock in the first place advised me that fantastic developments were expected. As usual, no fantastic developments took place, and after five months in New York I gave up the unequal struggle. I sold my last Canadian stock, which I had bought for 19 cents, for 10 cents. In the meantime I had begun to wonder if the bigger jungle nearer home, the New York Stock Exchange, would not be easier to assail. I called a friend of mine, a New York theatrical agent, Eddie Elkort, and asked him if he knew a New York broker. He gave me the name of a man whom I will call Lou Keller.

THE FUNDAMENTALIST

Chapter 2

Entering Wall Street

I called Lou Keller. I told him who I was and what I wanted. Next day he sent me some papers to sign, and advised me that as soon as I returned them with a deposit I would have an account with his brokerage firm. When I received his notice something happened to me. Suddenly I began to feel that I was becoming part of the financial scene. I cannot describe Wall Street because I have never been there physically, but even its name had an almost mystical attraction for me.

Here everything was going to be serious and different. I now considered my Canadian induction period as pure crazy gambling that I would never repeat.

As I studied the long gray columns of stock market quotations in the New York papers, I felt I was about to enter a new and successful period in my life. This was not like the wildcat Canadian market with its quick tip-offs on gold strikes and uranium fields.

This was responsible business, the street of bank presidents and great industrial combines, and I prepared to enter it with proper reverence.

I intended to make a much more cautious and mature approach to the stock market. I added up my assets to see what I had to work with. I had started in the Canadian market with $11,000–my original BRILUND investment of $3,000 and profit of $8,000.

This had been reduced by $5,200 in the fourteen months of my Canadian operations. All I had left of the BRILUND money was $5,800.

This did not seem like enough money with which to approach Wall Street, so I decided to add to it. From the savings of my show business activities I raised my stake to $10,000. It was a good round figure, and I deposited this sum with the broker.

Then one day I decided to start trading. I rang Lou Keller and nonchalantly, trying to be the old financial hand, simply asked him what was good.

I realize now this inquiry was more suitable for a butcher, but Mr. Keller was equal to it. He suggested several "safe stocks." He also gave me the fundamental reasons why these stocks were "safe." While I did not understand, I listened intently to such explanations as dividend increase, stock-splits, improved earnings. Now this to me was the highest professional advice. This man earned his living on Wall Street, so obviously he knew. Besides, he only "suggested." He emphasized that the decision was "up to me." This made me feel important and in command.

When one or two of the stocks he gave me rose a few points almost immediately, I had no doubt of the excellence of the information I was receiving and my natural ability as a stock market operator to act on it. What I did not know was that I was practically smack in the middle of the biggest bull market the world had ever seen and it was quite difficult, unless you were extremely unlucky, not to show a little paper profit from time to time.

Here are three typical consecutive deals I concluded in the early part of 1954—deals which convinced me I was a natural in Wall Street. In this table as in all the following tables in this book, I have included commissions and taxes.

200 COLUMBIA PICTURES		
Bought at	20	($4,050.00)
Sold at	22⅞	($4,513.42)

Profit			$ 463.42

200 NORTH AMERICAN AVIATION

Bought at	24¼	($4,904.26)	
Sold at	26⅞	($5,309.89)	
Profit			$ 405.63

100 KIMBERLY-CLARK

Bought at	53½	($5,390.35)	
Sold at	59	($5,854.68)	
Profit			$ 464.33
Total Profit			$1,333.38

You will note that each of these transactions netted me just over $400. It was not a large sum, but three profits in a row amounting to

$1,333.38 in just a few weeks made me feel that these were smooth, simple operations and I was in control.

The feeling that I was operating with a profit in Wall Street, allied to a natural awe of the place, made me feel foolishly happy. I felt I was losing my Canadian amateur status and becoming a member of an inner circle. I did not realize my method had not improved—that I was simply using more pompous words to cover it. For instance, I no longer considered the broker's advice as tips, but as "information". As far as I was concerned, I had given up listening to tips and instead was receiving authentic news based on valid economic evidence.

The boat sailed happily along. Here are some of my transactions during April and May 1954:

	Bought	Sold
NATIONAL CONTINER	11	12 ⅜
TRI-CONTINENTAL WARRANTS	5⅛	6
ALLIS-CHALMERS	50¾	54⅞

BUCYRUS-ERIE	24¾	26¾
GENERAL DYNAMICS	43½	47¼
MESTA MACHINE	32	34
UNIVERSAL PICTURES	19⅝	22¾

Profits, profits, profits. My confidence was at its height. This was clearly not Canada. Here everything I touched turned to gold. By the end of May, my $10,000 had grown to $14,600.

Occasional setbacks did not bother me. I regarded them as slight, inevitable delays in the upward climb towards prosperity. Besides, whenever a trade was successful I praised myself; when I lost, I blamed it on the broker.

I continued to trade constantly. I telephoned my broker sometimes twenty times a day. If I did not conduct at least one transaction a day I did not feel I was fulfilling my role in the market. If I saw a new stock I wanted to have it. I reached out for fresh stocks like a child for new toys.

These transactions in which I was involved in Wall Street around July 1954 will show the energy I expended for very small returns:

200	AMERICAN BROADCASTING-PARAMOUNT		
Bought	100 at 16⅞	($1,709.38)	
	100 at 17½	($1,772.50)	
Sold at	17⅞	($3,523.06)	
Profit			$41.18
100	NEW YORK CENTRAL		
Bought at	21½	($2,175.75)	
Sold at	22½	($2,213.70)	
Profit			$37.95
100 GENERAL REFRACTORIES			
Bought at	24¾	($2,502.38)	
Sold at	24¾	($2,442.97)	
Loss		$59.41	

100 AMERICAN AIRLINES

Bought at	14¾	($1,494.75)	
Sold at	15	($1,476.92)	
Loss			$17.83
Total Profit			$79.13
Total Loss			$77.24

My net profit on these transactions was $1.89. The only person who was happy was my broker. According to the New York Stock Exchange rules, his commission on these ten transactions amounted to $236.65. Incidentally, my $1.89 profit did not include the price of my telephone calls.

In spite of this, only one thing really bothered me. Half the words my broker used concerning the stock market I did not understand. I did not like to show my ignorance, so I decided to read up on the subject. In addition to the financial columns in the New York daily papers, I began to read books about the stock market so I could talk on his level.

Slowly I became acquainted with a series of new words and was always trying to use them. I was fascinated by words like earnings, dividends, capitalization. I learned that "per-share earnings" means "the company's net profit divided by the number of shares outstanding" and that "listed securities" are "those stocks that are quoted on the New York and American Stock Exchanges."

I labored over definitions of stocks, bonds, assets, profits, yields.

There was plenty to read, because there are hundreds of books published about the stock market. More has been written about the stock market,for instance, than about many cultural subjects.

At this time I studied books like:

R. C. Effinger	ABC of Investing
Dice & Eiteman	The Stock Market
B. E. Schultz	The Securities Market: And How It Works

Leo Barnes	Your Investments
H. M. Gartley	Profit In The Stock Market
Curtis Dahl	Consistent Profits In The Stock Market
E. J. Mann	You Can Make Money In The Stock Market

Armed with my new vocabulary, and what seemed to me my growing knowledge, I became more ambitious. I felt the time had come to find another BRILUND. After all, somewhere there must be a big, sound Wall Street stock that could do as well for me as what I now considered a "little penny stock."

I started to subscribe to stock market services such as Moody's, Fitch, and Standard & Poor's. They gave me what seemed to me magnificent information—except that I did not understand any of it.

Some of the passages read like this:

"Promised expansion in consumer expenditures for durable goods, non- durables and services, plus a fairly pronounced improvement in productive efficiency, provide the base for rather good earnings and dividend improvement for companies whose earnings will reflect the favorable nature of these conditions. We expect continued irregularity to continue temporarily under the guise of which this new status of the market's preference will be implemented."

They were dignified, impressive, they told me everything I wanted to know—except which stock was going up like BRILUND.

As I read them, however, curiosity overcame me. I wanted to see what other stock-market services were saying. I saw in the papers that, as in Canada, for one dollar I could have a four-week trial subscription to certain services. Soon I found myself a trial-subscriber of almost every service that advertised.

I collected clippings from everywhere—daily papers, financial columns, book jackets. Whenever I saw a new financial service advertised, I immediately put my dollar in the mail.

As the releases arrived, I found to my great surprise that they often contradicted each other. Frequently, a stock that on service recommended for buying, another recommended for selling. I also found that the recommendations were almost always non-committal. They used terms like "Buy on reactions," or "Should be bought on dips." But none of them told me what I should consider a reaction or a dip.

I overlooked all this and read on avidly, hoping to uncover the secret of the stock-that-can-only-rise.

One day an advisory service which prided itself on giving information only five or six times a year, published a very glossy release, nearly a whole book, examining EMERSON RADIO. It compared this company favorably with the mighty R.C.A. It went deeply into EMERSON'S capitalization, sales volume, profits before tax, profits after tax, per share earnings, comparative price-earnings ratios.

I did not understand all of this, but I was very impressed by these erudite words and the analytical comparisons. They proved that EMERSON stock, which was selling around 12, should be worth 30 to 35, comparable to the price of R.C.A. at that time.

Naturally, I bought EMERSON. I paid 12½, which seemed a nice low bargain price for a stock, which the glossy booklet assured me, was worth 35. What happened? This sure-fire stock began to drift downwards. Puzzled, baffled, I sold it.

Now, I am certain that the serious Wall Street analyst who prepared this glossy booklet had nothing but the highest intentions, but I must record in the interest of truth that by the end of 1956, this stock was down to 5¾.

About that time I heard a saying which has been passed from mouth to mouth for generations in Wall Street, but to me was new: "You cannot go broke taking a profit." I was much impressed by this and I was burning to put it into operation. This is how I did it.

One of the market leaders early in February 1955 was KAISER ALUMINUM. On my broker's recommendation I bought 100 shares at 63⅜, paying $6,378.84 for the stock. It went up steadily, and at 75 I sold it. I received $7,453.29, which gave me a profit of $1,074.45 in less than one month.

Hoping for another quick profit, I switched into 100 BOEING at 83. I paid $8,343.30 for these shares. The stock almost immediately began to drop. Four days later I sold at 79⅞ for $7,940.05. My loss on the BOEING transaction was $403.25.

Trying to make up for the loss, I then bought MAGMA COPPER in the first week of April. It was selling at 89¾. I paid $9,018.98 for 100 shares. No sooner did I buy, than it started to drop. Two weeks later I sold it at 80^4 for $8,002.18. This gave me a loss of $1,016.80.

By this time KAISER ALUMINUM, which I had jumped out of in the first week of March, had moved up to 82. An advisory service was recommending it, so I switched back to it, buying 100 shares at that price. I paid $8,243.20.

Five minutes later it started to slide. Not wanting to risk a further loss, I sold at 81¾ and received $8,127.59. This meant that for five minutes of trading I lost $115.61, including commissions.

On the first KAISER deal I had made a profit of $1,074.45. The losses sustained by jumping in and out of the other stocks were $1.53 5.66. So the whole circular transaction, which began with KAISER and ended with KAISER, gave me a net loss of $461.21.

If I had stuck with KAISER from my original purchase at 63⅜ until my ultimate sale at 81¾, I would have had a profit of $1,748.75 instead of the loss of $461.21.

Here is another case. From November 1954 to March 1955 I was constantly jumping in and out of a stock called RAYONIER, which in an eight-month period went from approximately 50 to 100. These were my transactions in RAYONIER, 100 shares at a time:

November-December 1954

Bought at	53	($5,340.30)	
Sold at	58¼	($5,779.99)	
Profit			$ 439.69

February-March 1955

Bought at	63⅞	($6,428.89)	
Sold at	71⅝	($7,116.13)	
Profit			$ 687.24

March 1955

Bought at	72	($7,242.20)	
Sold at	74	($7,353.39)	
Profit			$111.19
Total Profit			$1,238.12

The profit I made on this series of trades amounted to $1,238.12. Then the old loss pattern repeated itself. In April 1955 I switched into MANATI SUGAR. I bought 1,000 shares at 8%, paying $8,508.80. Immediately afterwards it started a downward slide and I sold out at the varying prices of 7¾, 7⅝ and 7½. I received a total of $7,465.70, giving me a loss of $1,043.10. This left me with a net profit of $195.02 on the combined RAYONIER-MANATI operation.

However, if I had held my original November purchase of RAYONIER without constantly trying to take a profit, and sold it in April at 80, I would have had a profit of $2,612.48 instead of $195.02.

What did all this mean? I did not appreciate it at the time, but it was a classic refutation of: "You cannot go broke taking a profit." Of course you can.

Another stock market saying that began to fascinate me was "Buy Cheap, Sell Dear." This sounded even better. But where could I buy something cheap? As I searched for a bargain, I discovered the over-the- counter market, the market of unlisted securities. I knew from my books that in order to get its stock listed and traded on the stock exchanges a company has to observe very stringent financial regulations. I had read that this did not apply to over-the-counter stocks.

This market, therefore, seemed to me the perfect place to find a bargain. I naively believed that because these stocks were not listed, few people knew about them and I could buy them cheap. I hurriedly subscribed to a monthly booklet called Over-the-Counter Securities Review and started hunting.

I searched eagerly among the thousands and thousands of names for the bargains that seemed to be offered. I bought stocks like PACIFIC AIRMOTIVE, COLLINS RADIO, GULF SULPHUR, DOMAN HELICOPTER, KENNAMETAL, TEKOIL CORPORATION and some of the more obscure ones. What I did not know was that when I came to offer them for sale, some of these stocks stuck to my fingers like tar. I found it very difficult getting rid of them— and rarely at anything like the price I paid for them. Why? Because there was no rigid price discipline as there is for the listed securities; there were no specialists—professionals to assure a continuous and orderly market; there were no reports where one could see at what price a transaction took place. There were only the "Bid" and "Ask" prices. These, I discovered, were often very far apart. When I wanted to sell at 42, which was the quoted "Ask" price, I only found a buyer at 38, the quoted "Bid" price. I sometimes ended up at 40 but that was by no means certain.

When I stumbled into the over-the-counter market, all this was unknown to me. Fortunately, I quickly came to realize that this is a specialized field and is only lucrative for experts who really know something about the affairs of a particular company. I decided to give it up, and returned my attention to listed securities.

All this time, I never once questioned the truth of any Wall Street rumors. I had no way of knowing that they are just as ill-founded and dangerous as rumors in the Canadian or other markets.

What I believed to be solid information, piped straight from Wall Street, had the most sensational lure for me. Here are two typical cases that show the sort of information I gobbled up and acted upon.

One day a strong rumor floated into the market that BALD-WIN-LIMA- HAMILTON, a firm of railroad equipment manufacturers, had received an order to construct an atomic train. Wall Street acted on this at once. The stock shot up from 12 to over 20.

By the time I heard this startling information, the stock had risen to what later turned out to be its peak. I bought 200 shares at 24½. The purchase price was $4,954.50. I held the stock for two weeks and watched with utter unbelief as it slipped slowly back to 19¼. By then even I realized that something was wrong, and I sold it for a loss of $1,160.38. However, I had done the very best thing in my bewilderment. I could have fared much worse with that stock, since it later went down to a low of 12¼.

Another time my broker called me and said, "STERLING PRECISION will go to 40 before the end of the year." The stock was quoted at 8. He gave me the reason: "The company is buying up many more small prosperous companies and will grow into a giant in no time." He added that this was first-hand information.

To me that was sufficient. Why not? A Wall Street broker, who I thought could not possibly be wrong, had favored me with this authentic news. I could not give my buying order quickly enough. I decided, in view of the source of my information, to plunge big on this one, I bought 1,000 STERLING PRECISION at 77/8 paying $8,023.10. I sat back happily to watch it rocket toward 40. Far from rocketing to 40, it began to waver. Slowly it slid downwards. When it looked as though it would fall below 7, something had obviously gone wrong, so I sold the stock at 71/8 for $6,967.45. This piece of news showed me a loss of $1,055.65 in a few days. The stock subsequently touched a low of 41/8.

But these losses were more than offset by the great pride I felt in being part of Wall Street, and I constantly searched for new approaches. One day, reading The Wall Street Journal, I saw a column reporting stock transactions by officers and directors of listed companies. When I looked into this further I found out that, to prevent manipulations, the Securities and Exchange Commission required that officers and directors report whenever they bought or sold stocks of their own company. Now, that was something! Here was a way for me to know what the real "insiders" were doing. All I had to do was to follow them. If they were buying, I would buy. If they were selling, I would sell.

I tried this approach, but it did not work. By the time I found out about the insiders' transactions, it was always too late. Besides, I often found that insiders were human too. Like other investors, they often bought too late or sold too soon. I made another discovery. They might know all about their company but they did not know about the attitude of the market in which their stock was sold.

Through these and other experiences, however, certain conclusions began to emerge. As a baby repeatedly hearing the same words starts to learn them, so did I slowly start, through my trading experiences, to discern the outlines of some rules that I could apply?

They were:

1. I should not follow advisory services. They are not infallible, either in Canada or on Wall Street.

2. I should be cautious with brokers' advice. They can be wrong.

3. I should ignore Wall Street sayings, no matter how ancient and revered.

4. I should not trade "over the counter"—only in listed stocks where there is always a buyer when I want to sell.

5. I should not listen to rumors, no matter how well founded they may appear.

6. The fundamental approach worked better for me than gambling. I should study it.

I wrote out these rules for myself and decided to act accordingly. I went over my brokerage statements and it was then that I discovered a transaction that gave me a seventh rule and led to the events that immediately followed. I discovered that I owned a stock and did not know it.

The stock was VIRGINIAN RAILWAY and I had bought 100 shares in August 1954 at 29¾ for $3,004.88. I had bought it and forgotten it, simply because I was too busy on the telephone jumping in and out of dozens of stocks—sometimes making as little as 75 cents; other times frantically calling up about a sliding stock, trying to sell it before it dropped any lower.

VIRGINIAN RAILWAY had never given me a moment's anxiety, so I left it alone. It was like a good child that sat playing quietly in the corner while I worried and fretted about the behavior of a dozen bad children. Now that I saw its name—after having held it for eleven months—I hardly recognized it. It had been so quiet, it had gone completely out of my mind. I rushed to my stock tables. It was standing at 43½. This forgotten, calm, dividend-paying stock had been slowly rising. I sold it and received $4,308.56. Without any effort on my part, or even any anxiety, it had made me $1,303.68. It also made me dimly aware of what was to become my rule number

I should rather hold on to one rising stock for a longer period than juggle with a dozen stocks for a short period at a time.

But which stock will rise? How to find it by myself?

I decided to have a look at VIRGINIAN RAILWAY. What had caused its steady rise while other stocks were jumping about? I asked my broker for information. He told me that the company paid a good dividend and had a fine earnings record. Its financial position was excellent. Now I knew the reason for the steady rise. It was a fundamental reason. This convinced me of the Tightness of my fundamental approach.

I made up my mind to refine this approach. I read, studied, analyzed. I set out to find the ideal stock.

I thought that if I really studied the company reports I could find out all about a stock and decide whether it was a good investment. I began to learn all about balance sheets and income accounts. Words like "assets," "liabilities," "capitalization," and "write-offs" became commonplace in my vocabulary.

For months I puzzled over these problems. Night after night, for hours after my daily dealings, I pored over the statements of hundreds of companies. I compared their assets, their liabilities, their profit margins, their price-earnings ratios.

I thumbed through lists like:

» Stocks with top quality rating

» Stocks the experts like

» Stocks selling below book value

» Stocks with strong cash position

» Stocks that have never cut their dividend

Time and again, however, I was confronted with the same problem. When things looked perfect on paper, when balance sheets seemed right, the prospects bright, the stock market never acted accordingly.

For instance, when I carefully compared the financial position of some dozen textile companies and after much study decided that the balance sheets clearly indicated that AMERICAN VISCOSE and STEVENS were the best choices, it was very puzzling to me why another stock called TEXTRON advanced in price while my two selections did not. I found this pattern repeatedly in other industry groups.

Baffled and a little disconcerted, I wondered whether it would not be wiser to adopt the judgment of a higher authority about the merits of a company. I asked my broker whether there was such an authority. He recommended a widely used, serious, very reliable monthly service, which gives the vital data on several thousand stocks—the nature of their business, their price ranges for at least twenty years, their dividend payments, their financial structure and their per-share annual earnings. It also rates each stock according to relative degrees of safety and value. It fascinated me to see how this was done.

High Grade stocks whose dividend payments are considered relatively sure are rated:

AAA—Safest
AA—Safe
A—Sound

Investment Merit stocks that usually pay dividends:

BBB—Best of group
BB—Good
B—Fair

Lesser Grade stocks, paying dividends but future not sure:

CCC—Best of group
CC—Fair dividend prospects
C—Slight dividend prospects Lowest Grade stocks:

DDD—No dividend prospects
DD—Slight apparent value
D—No apparent value

I studied all these ratings very carefully. It seemed so very simple. There was no longer any need for me to analyze balance sheets and income accounts. It was all spelled out for me here, I had only to compare: A is better than B, C is better than D.

I was absorbed and happy with this new approach. To me it had the charm of cold science. No longer was I the plaything of frantic, worrying rumor. I was becoming the cool, detached financier.

I was sure I was laying the foundation of my fortune. I now felt competent and confident. I listened to no one, I asked no one for advice. I decided everything I had done before was as slaphappy as my Canadian gambling period. I felt all I now needed to achieve success was to set up my own comparison tables. This I did, spending many grave and serious hours at the task.

CHAPTER 3

My First Crisis

From my reading I knew that stocks —like herds, indeed—form groups according to the industry they represent and that stocks belonging to the same industry have the tendency to move together in the market, either up or down.

It seemed only logical to me that I should try to find through fundamental analysis:

a) The strongest industry group;

b) The strongest company within that industry group.

Then I should buy the stock of that company and hold on to it, for such an ideal stock must rise.

I started studying the personality of a stock in relation to its industry group. When I read the quotations of GENERAL MOTORS I automatically looked at those of CHRYSLER, STUDEBAKER and AMERICAN MOTORS. If I looked at KAISER ALUMINUM, my eye automatically glanced afterwards at REYNOLDS METALS, ALCOA, and ALUMINIUM LTD. Instead of reading the stock tables in A.. B.. C.. order, I always read them in industry groups.

Whenever a stock started to behave better than the market generally I immediately looked at the behavior of its brothers—stocks of the same industry group. If I found that its brothers also behaved well, I looked for the head of the family—the stock that was acting best, the leader. I figured if I could not make money with the leader, I would certainly not make money with the others.

How delighted and important I felt doing all this! This serious, scientific approach made me feel like a soon-graduating expert in finance. Besides, I felt this was more than mere theory. I was going to put all this into practice and make a lot of money.

I started by compiling earnings of whole industry groups like oils, motors, aircraft, steel. I compared their past earnings with their present earnings. Then I compared these earnings with the earnings of other industry groups. I carefully evaluated their profit margins, their price- earnings ratios, their capitalizations.

Finally, after a tremendous amount of sifting and concentrating, I decided that the steel industry was the vehicle, which would make me rich.

Having made this decision, I then examined the industry in the minutest detail. Once again I delved into my rating service.

I was determined to play safe, so I figured the stock to buy should be in the "A" range and should pay a high dividend. But I received a surprise. As I went into this I discovered that "A" ratings were extremely rare and were almost always for preferred stocks. They were relatively stable price-wise and rarely rose spectacularly. Obviously these were not for me.

I decided to have a look at the "B" range. Here the stocks looked fine and they were numerous. I selected the five best known of them and started to compare them with each other. I did this with the utmost thoroughness. I set up my comparison table like this:

Company	Rating	Price: End of June 1955	Price-earnings ratio	Earnings per share			Estimated 1955	
				1952	1953	1954	Earnings	Dividend
Bethlehem Steel	BB	142⅜	7.9	8.80	13.30	13.18	18.00	7.25
Inland Steel BB	BB	79⅜	8.3	4.85	6.90	7.92	9.50	4.25

U.S. Steel	BB	54⅜	8.4	2.27	3.78	3.23	6.50	2.15
Jones & Laughlin	B	41½	5.4	2.91	4.77	3.80	7.75	2.25
Republic Steel	B	47¼	8.5	3.61	4.63	3.55	5.50	2.50

As I looked at my table I began to feel a wave of excitement. My table, like a pointer on a scale, clearly pointed to one stock: JONES & LAUGHLIN. I could not imagine why no one had noticed it before. Everything about it was perfect.

- It belonged to a strong industry group.
- It had a strong B rating.
- It paid almost 6% dividend.
- Its price-earnings ratio was better than that of any other stock in the group.

A tremendous enthusiasm came over me. This undoubtedly was the golden key. I felt fortune within my grasp like a ripe apple. This was the stock to make me wealthy. This was a gilt-edge scientific certainty, a newer and greater BRILUND. It was sure to jump 20 to 30 points any moment.

I had only one great worry. That was to buy a large amount of it, quickly, before others discovered it. I was so sure of my judgment, based on my detailed study that I decided to raise money from every possible soubce.

I had some property in Las Vegas, bought out of many years of work as a dancer. I mortgaged it. I had an insurance policy. I took a loan on it. I had a long-term contract with the "Latin Quarter" in New York. I asked for an advance.

I did not hesitate for a moment. I had no doubts. According to my most scientific and careful researches, nothing could go wrong.

The 23rd of September, 1955,1 bought 1,000 shares of JONES & LAUGHLIN at 52¼ on margin, which at that time was 70%. The cost was $52,652.30 and I had to deposit $36,856.61 in cash. To raise this amount I had put up all my possessions as a guarantee.

All this I had done with the greatest confidence. Now there was nothing to do but sit back and wait until I would begin to reap the harvest of my foolproof theory.

On September 26th the lightning struck, JONES & LAUGHLIN began to drop.

I could not believe it. How could it be? This was the new BRILUND. This was going to make my fortune. It was no gamble; it was a completely detached operation, based on infallible statistics. Still the stock continued to drop.

I saw it fall and yet I refused to face reality. I was paralyzed. I simply did not know what to do. Should I sell? How could I? In my projection, based on my exhaustive studies, JONES & LAUGHLIN was worth at least $75 per share. It was just a temporary setback, I said to myself. There is no reason for the drop. It is a good sound stock; it will come back. I must hold on. And I held on and I held on.

As the days went by I became afraid to look at the quotations. I trembled when I telephoned my broker. I was scared when I opened my newspaper.

When after a three-point drop the stock rose a half-point, my hopes started to rise with it. This is the start of recovery, I said. My fears temporarily calmed. But the following day the stock resumed its downward slide. On October 10th, when it hit 44, blind panic set in. How much further would it drop? What should I do? My paralysis turned to terror. Every point the stock dropped meant another $1,000 loss to me. This was too much for my nerves. I decided to sell, and my account was credited with $43,583.12. My net loss was $9,069.18.

I was crushed, finished, destroyed. All my smug ideas about myself as the scientific Wall Street operator crumbled. I felt as though a great bear had shambled up to me and mauled me just when I was preparing to shoot it. Where was the science? What was the use of research? What had happened to my statistics?

It would be difficult for anyone to conceive the shattering effects of the blow. If I had been a wild gambler, I could have expected such a position. But I had done my best not to be one. I had labored long and hard. I had done everything possible to avoid a mistake. I had researched, analyzed, compared. I had based my decision on the most trustworthy fundamental information. And yet, the only result was that I was wrecked to the tune of $9,000.

Black despair filled me when I realized I would probably lose my Las Vegas property. The horror of bankruptcy stared me in the face. All my confidence, built up by a benevolent bull market and by my first quick success with BRILUND, deserted me. Everything had been proved wrong. Gambling, tips, information, research, investigation, whatever method I tried to be successful in the stock market, had not worked out. I was desperate. I did not know what to do. I felt I could not go on.

Yet I had to go on. I must save my property. I must find a way to recoup my losses.

For hours every day I studied the stock tables, feverishly searching for some solution. Like a condemned man in a cell, I watched all the active stocks to see if they offered any escape.

Finally my eye noticed something. It was a stock I had never heard of, called TEXAS GULF PRODUCING. It appeared to be rising. I knew nothing about its fundamentals and had heard no rumors about it. All I knew was that it was rising steadily, day after day. Would it be my salvation? I did not know, but I had to try. Much more in despair than in hope, as a last wild attempt to recoup my losses, I gave an order to buy 1,000 shares at prices ranging between 57 1/8 and 37½. The total cost was $37,586.26.

I held my breath as I anxiously watched its continued rise. When it hit 40, I had a compelling temptation to sell. But I hung on. For the first time in my stock-market career I refused to take a quick profit. I dared not—I had that $9,000 loss to make up.

I telephoned my broker every hour, sometimes every fifteen minutes. I literally lived with my stock. I followed its every movement, every fluctuation. I was watching it the way an anxious parent watches over his newborn child.

For five weeks I held it, tensely watching it all the time.

Then one day, when it was standing at 43¼, I decided not to stretch my luck any further. I sold it and received $42,840.43. I had not got my $9,000 back, but I had recovered more than half of it.

When I sold TEXAS GULF PRODUCING I felt as if I had just passed the crisis in a long, critical illness. I was exhausted, empty, spent. And yet, something began to shine through. It came in the form of a question.

What, I asked myself, was the value of examining company reports, studying the industry outlook, the ratings, the price-earnings ratios? The stock that saved me from disaster was one about which I knew nothing. I picked it for one reason only— it seemed to be rising.

Was this the answer? It could be.

So the unfortunate experience with JONES & LAUGHLIN had its significance. It was not wasted. It led me toward the glimmering of my theory.

THE TECHNICIAN

Chapter 4

Developing the Box Theory

After my frightening experience with JONES & LAUGHLIN, and my more fortunate experience with TEXAS GULF PRODUCING, I sat down to assess my position. By now I had been scared and beaten by the market enough to appreciate that I should not regard the stock market as a mysterious machine from which, if I were lucky, fortunes could be extracted like the jackpot in a slot machine. I realized that although there is an element of chance in every field in life, I could not base my operations on luck. I could be lucky once, maybe twice—but not constantly.

No, this was not for me. I must rely on knowledge. I must learn how to operate in the market. Could I win at bridge without knowing the rules? Or in a chess game without knowing how to answer my opponent's moves? In the same way, how could I expect to succeed in the market without learning how to trade? I was playing for money, and the game in the market was against the keenest experts. I could not play against them and expect to win without learning the fundamentals of the game.

And so I started. First I examined my past experiences. On one hand, using the fundamental approach, I was wrong. On the other hand, using the technical approach, I was right. Obviously the best method was to try to repeat the successful approach I had used with TEXAS GULF PRODUCING.

It was not easy. I sat with my stock tables for hours each evening, trying to find another stock like it. Then one day I noticed a stock called M & M WOOD WORKING. None of the financial information services could tell me anything much about it. My broker had never heard of it. Yet I remained obstinately interested because its daily action reminded me of TEXAS GULF PRODUCING. I started to watch it carefully.

In December 1955 the stock rose from about 15 to 23⅝ at the year end. After a five-week lull, its trading volume increased and its price resumed its advance. I decided to buy 500 shares at 26⅝. It continued to rise and I held on, watching its movement intently. It kept moving upward and its volume of trading was consistently high. When it reached 33,1 sold it and took a profit of $2,866.62.

I was happy and excited—not so much because of the money but simply because I had bought M & M WOOD WORKING, as I had bought TEXAS GULF PRODUCING, purely on the basis of its action in the market. I knew nothing about it nor could I find out very much. Yet I assumed from its continuing rise and high volume that some people knew a lot more about it than I did.

This proved to be correct. After I had sold it, I found out from the newspaper that the steady rise had been due to a merger, which was being secretly negotiated. It was eventually revealed that a not h er com pa ny planned t o take o ver M & M WOOD WORKING for $35 a share, and this offer was accepted. This also meant that although I was in complete ignorance about the behind-the-scene deal, I had only sold out 2 points under the high. I was fascinated to realize that my buying, based purely on the stock's behavior, enabled me to profit from a proposed merger without knowing anything about it. I was an insider without actually being one.

This experience did more than anything to convince me that the purely technical approach to the market was sound. It meant that if I studied price action and volume, discarding all other factors, I could get positive results.

I now began to try to work from this point of view. I concentrated on a close study of price and volume and tried to ignore all rumors, tips or fundamental information. I decided not to concern myself with the reasons behind a rise. I figured that if some fundamental change for the better takes place in the life of a company, this soon shows up in the rising price and volume of its stock, because many people are anxious to buy it. If I could train my eyes to spot this upward change in its early stages, as in the case of M & M WOOD WORKING, I could participate in the stock's rise without knowing the reason for it.

The problem was: How to detect this change? After much thinking I found one criterion—that was to compare stocks with people.

This is how I began to work it out: If a tempestuous beauty were to jump on a table and do a wild dance, no one would be particularly astonished. That is the sort of characteristic behavior people have come to expect from her. But if a dignified matron were suddenly to do the same, this would be unusual and people would immediately say, "There is something strange here— something has happened. *'

In the same way, I decided that if a usually inactive stock suddenly became active I would consider this unusual, and if it also advanced in price I would buy it. I would assume that somewhere behind the out- of-the-ordinary movement there was a group who had some good information. By buying the stock I would become their silent partner.

I tried this approach. Sometimes I was successful, sometimes not. What I did not realize was that my eyes were not sufficiently trained yet, and exactly when I started to feel confident I could operate on my theory, I was in for a rude awakening.

In May 1956 I noticed a stock called PITTSBURGH METALLURGICAL, which at that time was quoted at 67, It was a fast-moving, dynamic stock and I thought it would continue to move up rapidly. When I saw its increased activity, I bought 200 shares for a total cost of $13,483.40.

I was so sure of my judgment that I threw all caution overboard and when the stock—contrary to my expectation—began to weaken, I thought this was just a small reaction. I was sure that after the slight drop it was set for another big upward move. The move was there all right—but it was in the wrong direction. Ten days later PITTSBURGH METALLURGICAL stood at 57¾. I sold it. My loss was $2,023.32.

Something was obviously wrong. Everything clearly pointed to the stock as the best in the market at that time and still, no sooner had I bought it, than it dropped. And what was more disillusioning, no sooner did I sell it than it started to move up.

Trying to find an explanation, I examined the stock's previous movements and discovered that I had bought it at the top of an 18- point rise. This was as much as the stock could contain for the time being. Almost at the very point that I put money in it, it started to drift downward. It was evident that I had bought the right stock at the wrong time.

Looking back I could see this very clearly. I could see exactly why the stock had performed the way it did—afterwards. The question, however, was: How to judge a movement at the time it happens?

It was a simple, straightforward problem, but it was complex in its enormity. I already knew that book systems did not help, balance sheets were useless information was suspect and wrong.

Clutching at a straw, I decided to make an extensive study of individual stock movements. How do they act? What are the characteristics of their behavior? Is there any pattern in their fluctuations?

I read books, I examined stock tables, I inspected hundreds of charts. As I studied them I began to learn things about stock movements which I had not seen before. I started to realize that stock movements were not completely haphazard. Stocks did not fly like balloons in any direction. As if attracted by a magnet, they had a defined upward or downward trend, which, once established, tended to continue. Within this trend stocks moved in a series of frames, or what I began to call "boxes".

They would oscillate fairly consistently between a low and a high point. The area, which enclosed this up-and-down movement, represented the box or frame. These boxes began to exist very clearly for me.

This was the beginning of my box theory, which was to lead to a fortune.

This is how I applied my theory: When the boxes of a stock in which I was interested stood, like a pyramid, on top of each other, and my stock was in the highest box, I started to watch it. It could bounce between the top and the bottom of the box and I was perfectly satisfied. Once I had decided on the dimensions of the box, the stock could do what it liked, but only within that frame. In fact, if it did not bounce up and down inside that box I was worried.

No bouncing, no movement, meant it was not a lively stock. And if it were not a lively stock I was not interested in it because that meant it would probably not rise dynamically.

Take a stock, which was within the 45/50 box. It could bounce between those figures as often as it liked and I would still consider buying it. If, however, it fell to 44½, I eliminated it as a possibility.

Why? Because anything below 45 meant it was falling back into a lower box and this was all wrong—I wanted it only if it was moving into a higher box.

I found that a stock sometimes stayed for weeks in one box. I did not care how long it stayed in its box as long as it did and did not fall below the lower frame figure.

I observed, for instance, that when a stock was in the 45/50 box it might read like this:

45. 47 - 49. 50 - 45 - 47

This meant that, after reaching a high at 50, it could react to a low at 45 then close every day at 46 or 47 and I was quite happy. It was still within its box. But, of course, the movement I was constantly watching for was an upward thrust toward the next box. If this occurred I bought the stock.

I did not find any fixed rule as to how this takes place. It just has to be observed and instantly acted upon. Some volatile, eager stocks moved into another box within hours. Others took days. If the stock acted right, it started to push from its 45/50 box into another, upper box. Then its movement began to read something like this:

48 - 52 - 50 - 55 - 51 - 50 - 53 - 52

It was now quite clearly establishing itself in its next box—the 50/55 box.

Do not misunderstand me on this. These are only examples. What I had to decide was the range of the box. This, of course, varied with different stocks. For instance, some stocks moved in a very small frame, perhaps not more than 10% each way. Other wide-swinging stocks moved in a frame between 15% and 20%. The task was to define the frame exactly and be sure the stock did not move decisively below the lower edge of the box. If it did, I sold it at once, because it was not acting right.

While it stayed within its box, I considered a reaction from 55 to 50 as quite normal. It did not mean to me that the stock was going to fall back. Just the contrary.

Before a dancer leaps into the air he goes into a crouch to set himself for the spring. I found it was the same with stocks. They usually did not suddenly shoot up from 50 to 70. In other words, I considered that a stock in upward trend that reacted to 45 after reaching 50 was like a dancer crouching, ready for the spring-up.

Later when I had more experience I also learned that this 45 position in a stock after a 50 high point has another important benefit. It shakes out the weak and frightened stockholders who mistake this reaction for a drop, and enables the stock to advance more rapidly.

I came to see that when a stock was on a definite upward trend there was a feeling of proportion about its advance. If it was on its way, rising from, let us say, 50 to 70 but occasionally dropping back that was all part of the right rhythm.

It might have gone like this:

50 - 52 - 57 - 58 - 60 - 55 - 52 – 56

That meant it was in the 52/60 box.

After this, on an upward swing, it might have gone: 58- 61 - 66 - 70 - 66 - 63 - 66

This meant it was well inside the 63/70 box. I also considered that it was still edging towards higher spheres.

The major problem still remained; what was the right time to buy into it? Logically, it was the moment when it entered a new higher box. This seemed quite simple, until the case of LOUISIANA LAND & EXPLORATION proved it was not.

For weeks I watched the behavior of this stock and saw it form its pyramiding boxes. When the upper frame of its last box was 59¾ I felt I had assessed it correctly. I told the broker to telephone me when it reached 61, which I considered the door of its new box. He did, but I was not in my hotel room when the call came. It took him two hours to reach me. By the time he did, the stock was quoted at 63. I was disappointed. I felt I had been deprived of a great opportunity.

I was angry at the way it had passed me at 61 and when it went to 63 in such a short time I was certain I had missed a very good thing. Good reason deserted me in my excitement. I would have paid any price for this stock in my enthusiasm. I just had to get into a stock, which I thought was going up to a fabulous price.

Up it went—63½—64½—65. I was right. I had judged it correctly and I had missed it! I could not wait any longer. I bought

100 shares at 65—at the top of its new box—because I had missed it at the bottom.

Although I was improving in my selection and method, I was still somewhat of a baby in the mechanics of Wall Street, so I placed my problem before the broker. We discussed the 61-point telephone call, which had unfortunately missed me. He told me I should have put in an automatic "on stop" buy order. This meant the stock would have been bought when it rose to 61. He suggested that whenever I made a decision about a stock I should put in a buy order at a named figure. Then the stock would be bought for me without further consultation if the market reached this figure. This I agreed to do.

My problem of buying automatically at what I thought was the right time was settled.

By this time my box theory and its form of application were firmly planted in my mind and on three consecutive occasions I used it successfully.

I bought ALLEGHENY LUDLUM STEEL when it appeared to me to be going into the 45/50 box. I bought 200 shares at 45¾ and sold them three weeks later at 51.

I also bought 300 shares of DRESSER INDUSTRIES when it seemed to be entering the 84/92 box. I bought at 84, but as it did not seem to be making the right progress through the box, I sold at 86½.

Then I bought 300 shares of COOPER-BESSEMER at the bottom edge of the 45/50 box at 40¾ and sold at 45½.

My profit on these three transactions was $2,442.36.

This gave me a great deal of confidence, but then I received a slap in the face, which proved to me that I needed more than a theory alone. In August I bought 500 shares of NORTH AMERICAN AVIATION at 94⅜ because I was sure it was about to establish itself in a new box over 100. It did not. Almost immediately it turned around and started to fall back. I could have sold it when it gave up a point. I could have done the same when it lost another point. But I decided against it and stubbornly held on. My pride did not let me act. The prestige of my theory was at stake. I just kept saying this stock cannot go down any further. I did not know what I learned later, that there is no such thing as cannot in the market. Any stock can do anything. By the end of the next week, the profit from my three previous operations was gone. I was back where I had started.

1. This experience, as I see it, was an important turning point of my stock-market career.

2. It was at this point that I finally realized that

3. There is no sure thing in the market - I was bound to be wrong half of the time.

4. I must accept this fact and readjust myself accordingly - my pride and ego would have to be subdued.

5. I must become an impartial diagnostician, who does not identify himself with any theory or stock.

6. I cannot merely take chances. First, I have to reduce my risks as far as humanly possible.

The first step I took in that direction was to adopt what I called my quick-loss weapon. I already knew that I would be wrong half of the time. Why not accept my mistakes realistically and sell immediately at a small loss? If I bought a stock at 25, why not at the same time order the stock to be sold if it returned below 24?

I decided to give "on-stop" orders to buy at a certain figure with an automatic "stop-loss" order on them in case the stock went down. This way, I figured, I would never sleep with a loss. If any of my stocks went below the price I thought they should, I would not own them when I went to bed that night. I knew that many times I would be "stopped out" for the sake of a point just to see my stock climb up immediately after. But I realized that this was not so important as stopping the big losses. Besides, I could always buy back the stock—by paying a higher price.

Then I took the second equally important step.

I knew that being right half of the time was not the answer to success. I began to understand how I could break even and still go broke. If I invested about $10,000 and I operated in a medium-priced stock, each operation would cost me approximately $125 in commission every time I bought a stock, and another $125 every time I sold it.

Let us suppose I was right half of the time. At $250 a deal, I had only to trade 40 times without taking a real loss and I had lost my capital. It would be completely eroded by commissions. This is how the commission-mice would nibble away at each operation and would finally eat up my money:

Bought	500 shares at $20	
PAID (including commission)		$10,125.00
Sold	500 shares at $20	
RECEIVED (deducting commission)		$ 9,875.00
LOSS		$ 250.00
40 transactions at $250 = $10,000		

There was only one answer to this danger: My profits had to be bigger than my losses.

I had learned from experience that my most difficult problem was to discipline myself not to sell a rising stock too quickly. I always sold too quickly because I am a coward. Whenever I bought a stock at 25 and it rose to 30, I became so worried it might go back that I sold it. I knew the right thing to do but I invariably did the opposite.

I decided that since I could not train myself not to get scared every time, it was better to adopt another method. This was to hold on to a rising stock but, at the same time, keep raising my stop-loss order parallel with its rise. I would keep it at such a distance that a meaningless swing in the price would not touch it off. If, however, the stock really turned around and began to drop, I would be sold out immediately. This way the market would never be able to get more than a fraction of my profits away.

And how to determine when to take profits?

I realized that I would not be able to sell at the top. Anyone who claims he can consistently do this is lying. If I sold while the stock was rising, it would be a pure guess, because I could not know how far an advance might carry. This would be no cleverer a guess than anticipating that "My Fair Lady" would end its run after 200 performances. You could also guess it would go off after 300 or 400 performances. Why did it not go off at any of these figures? Because the producer would be a fool to close the show when he sees the theater full every night. It is only when he starts to notice empty seats that he considers closing the show.

I carried the Broadway comparison through to the problem of selling. I would be a fool to sell a stock as long as it keeps advancing. When to sell then? Why, when the boxes started to go into reverse! When the pyramids started to tumble downwards, that was the time to close the show and sell out. My trailing stop-loss, which I moved up behind the rising price of the stock, should take care of this automatically.

Having made these decisions, I then sat back and re-defined my objectives in the stock market:

1. Right stocks
2. Right timing
3. Small losses
4. Big profits

I examined my weapons:

1. Price and volume
2. Box theory
3. Automatic buy-order
4. Stop-loss sell-order

As to my basic strategy, I decided I would always do this: I would just jog along with an upward trend, trailing my stop-loss insurance behind me. As the trend continued, I would buy more. When the trend reversed? I would run like a thief.

I realized that there were a great many snags. There was bound to be a lot of guesswork in the operation. My estimate that I would be right half of the time could be optimistic. But at last I saw my problem more clearly than ever. I knew that I had to adopt a cold, unemotional attitude toward stocks; that I must not fall in love with them when they rose and I must not get angry when they fell; that there are no such animals as good or bad stocks. There are only rising and falling stocks—and I should hold the rising ones and sell those that fall.

I knew that to do this I had to achieve something much more difficult than anything before. I had to bring my emotions— fear, hope and greed—under complete control. I had no doubt that this would require a great amount of self-discipline, but I felt like a man who knew a room could be lit up and was fumbling for the switches.

■ □ ■ □ $ □ ■ □ ■

Chapter 5

Cables Round the World

Almost at the same time that I started to operate with my new principles in mind, I signed up to make a two-year tour of the world with my dancing act. Immediately, I was faced with many problems. How, for instance, could I continue to trade while I was at the other side of the world? And instantly and very vividly there came before my mind the occasion when my broker missed me on the telephone. If this could happen in New York, how was I to overcome such a difficulty when I was thousands of miles away? I discussed the matter with him and we decided that we could remain in touch with each other through cables.

We also decided upon one tool—this was Barton's, a weekly financial publication, which we arranged to have airmailed to me as soon as it was published. This would show me any stocks, which might be moving up. At the same time a daily telegram would quote the stocks I owned. Even in such remote places as Kashmir and Nepal, where I performed during the tour, the daily telegram duly arrived. It contained the Wall Street closing prices of my stocks.

To save time and money, I had instituted a special code with my broker in New York. My cables consisted only of a string of letters denoting the stocks, each followed by a series of apparently meaningless numbers. They looked something like this:

"B 32½ L 57 U 89½ A 120¼ F 132¼"

It only took me a few days to discover that these quotations were insufficient for me to properly follow the movements of my stocks. I was unable to construct my boxes without knowing the upper and lower limits of their moves. I called New York and asked my broker to add to each closing price the full details of the stock's daily price fluctuations. This consisted of the highest and lowest price of the stock for that day. Now my telegrams started to look like this:

"B 32½ (34½-32⅜) L 57 (58⅝-57 U 89½ (91½-89) A 120¼ (121/2-120¼) F 132¼ (134⅞-132¼)."

I did not ask for volume quotes, as I feared that too many figures might overcrowd my cables. My selections were high-volume stocks anyway and I thought that if the volume contracted, I would notice it in Barron's a few days later.

As my broker and I both knew which stocks we were quoting, we only used the first letter of the name of each stock I owned. But because these were not the normal stock-market abbreviations which are known all over the world, these constant mysterious letter-figure cables upset and bothered post-office employees almost everywhere. Before they handed my first cables to me, I had to give them a detailed explanation of what they contained.

They obviously thought I must be a secret agent. I was constantly confronted with this suspicion, especially in the Far East. It was perhaps worst in Japan. The telegraph officials there were more suspicious than anywhere else, as the Japanese bureaucrats do not appear to have completely shed their pre-war spy mania. Whenever I went to a new town such as Kyoto, Nagoya or Osaka, the cable officials would look at me with the gravest doubts.

I had always to go into long explanations. As I did not speak Japanese, this was often a complicated operation. Oddly enough, however, they seemed quite happy as soon as I signed a paper telling them exactly what my cables contained. It might not have been the truth, but that did not seem to have occurred to them. On the other hand, without this paper bearing my signature, they would refuse to send my cables.

It took me a long time to change their minds. I spent six months in Japan before I finally became a well-known figure in the cable offices of most of the major cities. They even began cheerfully to accept my cables without a special signature. The word had gone around among the Japanese that I was a mad, but apparently harmless, European who kept sending and receiving telegrams containing financial gibberish.

During my tour of the world my journeys ranged from Hong Kong to Istanbul, Rangoon, Manila, Singapore, Stockholm, Formosa, Calcutta, Japan and many other places. Naturally I often ran into other difficulties trying to receive or send my cables.

One major problem was that while I was traveling I had to be careful that cables did not miss me. So when I was on the move they were duplicated or even triplicated. It was quite common for the same cable to leave Wall Street addressed Pan-Am Flight 2 Hong Kong Airport, repeated Tokyo Airport, repeated Nikkatsu Hotel Tokyo. This arrangement enabled me, if I missed it in flight, to pick it up immediately after landing.

My difficulties in operating in Wall Street from Vientiane in Laos, for instance, were tremendous. The first of them was that there was no telephone system there at all. The only local telephone was between the American military mission and the American Embassy, which, of course, was of no use to me.

If I wanted to send or collect any messages I had to take a rickshaw to the post office, which was open just eight hours a day and always closed bang on the minute.

Since there was a difference of twelve hours between local and New York time, the post office was shut from opening to closing time on Wall Street. I was under constant tension, worrying whether important news from the stock market was being held up.

One day when I went to the post office, I found a telegram awaiting me, which had been forwarded from Saigon to Hong Kong and then sent on from Hong Kong to Vientiane. I opened it apprehensively, thinking that the delay certainly must spell disaster. But luckily it contained no information I felt compelled to act upon.

But Laos was only one of the places where I ran into difficulties. In Kathmandu, the capital of Nepal in the Himalayas, there was no telegraph service at all. The only telegraph office was in the Indian Embassy and all communications by cable from the outside world came through there.

The Embassy officials obviously considered it beneath their dignity to bother about private cables addressed to ordinary people. When a telegram arrived for me they would not deliver it, and I had to constantly telephone the Embassy to see if there were any messages. Sometimes I had to call ten times before they told me to come and collect my cables. Moreover, they were handwritten and often illegible.

The basic mechanics of my operations were these: Barron's, published in Boston on Mondays, usually reached me if I was in Australia or India, or any part of the world not too remote, by Thursday. This, of course, meant that I was four days behind the Wall Street movements. However, when I saw in Barron's a stock that behaved according to my theories, I sent a telegram to my broker asking him to bring me up to date on the stock's movements from Monday to Thursday, for example:

"CABLE THIS WEEK'S RANGE AND CLOSE CHRYSLER."

If the stock, for instance, was, in my opinion, behaving well in the 60/65 box, I would wait to see if the four-day quotations from New York still showed this. If the quotations cabled to me showed it was still in this box, I decided to watch it. I would then ask my broker to quote it daily so I could see if it was pressing toward a higher box. If I was satisfied with what I saw, I cabled to New York my on stop buy order, which my broker was instructed to consider good-till-cancelled unless otherwise specified. This was always coupled with an automatic stop-loss order in case the stock dropped after I bought it. A typical cable looked like this:

"BUY 200 CHRYSLER 67 ON STOP 65 STOPLOSS."

If, on the other hand, my broker's cable showed it had moved out of the 60/65 box. Since I had noticed it in Barron's, I forgot about it. It was too late for me to act. I had to wait for another opportunity.

Naturally, I was forced to narrow down my operations to a few stocks. The reason was purely financial. If I spent more than $12 to $15 a day on cables requesting stock quotations, the operation would become uneconomic unless I made enormous profits.

In the beginning, I was terribly afraid. Not that being in New York had helped me in the past, but to be able to communicate with Wall Street by telephone had given me a false feeling of security. This I missed for a while. It was only later, as I gradually gained experience in trading through cables, that I came to see the advantages of it. No phone calls, no confusion, no contradictory rumors—these factors combined gave me a much more detached view.

As I only handled five to eight stocks at a time, I automatically separated them from the confusing, jungle-like movement of the hundreds of stocks, which surrounded them. I was influenced by nothing but the price of my stocks.

I could not hear what people said, but I could see what they did. It was like a poker game in which I could not hear the betting, but I could see all the cards.

I did not know it at the time, but later, as I became more experienced in the market, I realized how invaluable this was to me. Of course, the poker players would try to mislead me with words, and they would not show me their cards. But if I did not listen to their words, and constantly watched their cards, I could guess what they were doing.

At first I tried to practice on paper without investing any money. But I soon discovered that working on paper was quite different from actual investing. It was like playing cards without any dollars in the pot. It had as much savor and excitement as bridge at an old ladies' home.

Everything seemed very easy on paper with no money at stake. But as soon as I had $ 10,000 invested in a stock the picture became quite different. With no money involved I could easily control my feelings, but as soon as I put dollars into a stock my emotions came floating quickly up to the surface.

As my cables continued to arrive day after day, I slowly became accustomed to this new type of operation and started to feel more and more confident. Only one particular fact bothered me. Sometimes some of my stocks made inexplicable moves, which had no relation to their previous behavior.

This baffled me, and it was while I was looking for an explanation that I made a momentous discovery. I realized I was on my own. I was certain I could learn nothing more from books. No one could guide me. I was completely alone with my daily telegrams and my weekly issues of Barton's. They were my only contact with Wall Street, many thousands of miles away. If I wanted an explanation, I could only turn to them.

So I plunged avidly into Barron's. I turned its pages until they turned to shreds before I finally discovered this: the inexplicable moves in my stocks usually coincided with some violent move in the general market. As I only received the quotes of my own stocks, I was completely disregarding the possible influence of the general market on them. This was no better than trying to direct a battle by only looking at one section of the battlefield.

This was a very important discovery for me and I immediately acted on it. I asked my broker to add to the end of my cables the closing price of the Dow-Jones Industrial Average. This I thought would give me a clear enough picture of how the general market behaved.

My telegrams now read like this:

"B 32½ (34½-32⅜) L 57 (58⅝-57) U 89½ (91½-89) A

120¼ (121½-120¼) F 132¼ (134⅞-132¼) 482.31"

When I received the first cables with this added information, I was like a child with a new toy. I thought I had discovered a completely new formula. As I tried to relate the Dow-Jones Industrial Average to the movements of my own stocks, I reasoned that if the Average was going up, so would my stocks.

Soon after, I found out that this was not true. To try to fit the market into a rigid pattern was a mistake. It seemed quite impossible to do it. Each stock behaved differently. There was no such thing as a mechanical pattern. I was wrong many times before I banished the Average to its proper place. It was some time before I discovered that the Dow-Jones Company publishes an average. It simply mirrors the day-to-day behavior of 3 0 selected stocks. Other stocks are influenced by it but do not mechanically follow its pattern. I also began to appreciate that the Dow-Jones Company is not a fortune-telling organization. It does not attempt to tell you when individual stocks will rise or fall.

Gradually, I began to understand that I could not apply mechanical standards to the relationship between the Average and individual stocks. Judging this relationship was much more like an art. In some ways it was like painting. An artist puts colors on a canvas obeying certain principles, but it would be impossible for him to explain how he does it. In the same way I found that the relationship between the Average and my individual stocks were confined within certain principles, but they could not be measured exactly. From then on, I made up my mind to keep watching the Dow-Jones Industrial Average, but only in order to determine whether I was in a strong or a weak market. This I did because I realized that a general market cycle influences almost every stock. The main cycles like a bear or a bull market usually creep into the majority of them.

Now that I was armed with a finishing touch to my theory, I felt much stronger. I felt as though I was beginning to touch some of the light switches, which would illuminate the room.

I discovered I could form an opinion on the stocks from the

telegrams in front of me. They became like X-rays to me. To the uninitiated, an X-ray picture is meaningless. But to a physician, it often contains all the information he wants to know. He relates its findings to the nature and duration of the illness, the age of the patient, etc., and only then does he draw his conclusions.

Looking at my telegrams, I did something similar. I compared the prices of my stocks first with each other, then with the Dow-Jones Average, and after I weighed their trading range, I evaluated whether I should buy, sell or hold.

I did this automatically without deeper analysis. I could not fully explain this to myself until I realized that I was now reading and no longer spelling out the alphabet. I was doing what an educated adult does—I could absorb the printed page at a glance and draw rapid conclusions from it, instead of painfully putting the letters together like a child.

Simultaneously, I tried to train my emotions. I worked it this way: Whenever I bought a stock, I wrote down my reason for doing so. I did the same when I sold it. Whenever a trade ended with a loss, I wrote down the reason I thought caused it. Then I tried not to repeat the same mistake. This is how one of my tables looked:

	Brought	Sold	Cause of Error
ISLAND CREEK COAL	46	43½	Brought too late
JOY MANUFACTURING	62	60⅝	Stop-loss too close
EASTERN GAS & FUEL	27¾	25⅛	Overlooked weak general market
ALCOA	118	116½	Brought on decline
COOPER-BESSEMER	55⅜	54	Wrong timing.

These cause-of-error tables helped me immeasurably. As I drew them up one after the other I was learning something from each trading. I started to see that stocks have characters just like people. This is not so illogical, because they faithfully reflect the character of the people who buy and sell them.

Like human beings, stocks behave differently. Some of them are calm, slow, conservative. Others are jumpy, nervous, tense. Some of them I found easy to predict. They were consistent in their moves, logical in their behavior. They were like dependable friends.

And some of them I could not handle. Each time I bought them they did me an injury. There was something almost human in their behavior. They did not seem to want me. They reminded me of a man to whom you try to be friendly but who thinks you have insulted him and so he slaps you. I began to take the view that if these stocks slapped me twice I would refuse to touch them any more. I would just shake off the blow and go away to buy something I could handle better. This does not mean, of course, that other people with a different temperament from mine were not able to get on well with them - just as some people get along with one set of people better than they do with others.

The experience I gained through my cause-of-error tables became one of the most important of all my qualifications. I now realized I could never have learned it from books. I began to see that it is like driving a car. The driver can be taught how to use the accelerator, the steering wheel and the brakes, but he still has to develop his own feeling for driving. No one can tell him how to judge whether he is too close to the car in front of him or when he should slow down. This he can only learn through experience.

As I flew around the world and operated in Wall Street by cables, I slowly came to see that though I was becoming a diagnostician I could not be a prophet. When I examined a stock and found it strong, all I could say was: It is healthy now, today, at this hour. I could not guarantee it would not catch a cold tomorrow. My educated guesses, no matter how cautious they were, many times turned out to be wrong. But this did not upset me any more. After all, I thought, who was I to say what a stock should or should not do?

Even my mistakes did not make me unhappy. If I was right, so much the better. If I was wrong—I was sold out. This happened automatically as something apart from me. I was no longer proud if the stock went up, nor did I feel wounded if it fell. I knew now that the word "value" cannot be used in relation to stocks. The value of a stock is its quoted price. This in turn is entirely dependent on supply and demand. I finally learned that there is no such thing as a $50 stock. If a $50 stock went to $49—it was now a $49 stock. Being thousands of miles away from Wall Street, I succeeded in disassociating myself emotionally from every stock I held.

I also decided not to be influenced by the tax problem. Many people hold on to stocks for six months to obtain long-term capital gain. This I considered dangerous. I might lose money by holding on to a falling stock just for tax reasons.

I decided I would trade in the market by doing the right thing first— follow what a stock's behavior commands and care about taxes later.

As if stocks were made to confirm my new attitude, I handled them successfully for quite a while. I bought with bold confidence when I thought I was right and coldly, without hurt ego, I took my limited losses when I thought I was proven wrong.

One of my most successful operations was in COOPER-BESSEMER. I bought three times into this stock, each time 200 shares. Two operations ended with a loss, but the third made me a sizeable profit. Here are the details of these purchases:

November 1956

Brought at	46	($9,276.00)	
Sold at	45⅛	($8,941.09)	
			Loss $334.91

December 1956

Brought at	55⅜	($11,156.08)	
Sold at	54	($10,710.38)	
			Loss $445.70

January – April 1957

Brought at	57	($11,481.40)	
Sold at	70¾	($14,056.95)	
			Profit $2,575.55

A few other stocks, like DRESSER INDUSTRIES and REYNOLDS METALS, behaved equally well and gave me satisfactory profits.

But then, in the summer of 1957, when I was in Singapore, a most staggering series of events developed.

I brought BALTIMORE & OHIO RAILROAD at 56¼. I thought it was in the 56/61 box and it would advance. But it started reaching down, and I sold it at 55.

Then I tried DOBECKMUN. I judged it was in a 44/49 box, so I brought it at 45. It began to sag and I sold it at 41.

I brought DAYSTROM at 44 because I thought it was rising into the 45/50 box. I sold out at 42¼.

I brought FOSTER WHEELER at 61¾. I thought it was in the 60/80 box. When it turned slowly against me, I sold out just below 60 frame at 59½.

AEROQUIP was the last one. I had brought it at prices ranging from 23¼ to 27⅝. I watched it climb towards 30 and waited for the 31/35 box to evolve. It did not happen that way. I was stopped out of AEROQUIP at 27½.

Finally, on August 26, 1957, I found myself without a single stock. My automatic stop-loss had sold me out of everything. In two months every one of my stocks had slowly turned around, and one by one had sagged through the bottom of their boxes. And one by one, even if it was only a question of half a point, they were sold.

I did not like it, but there was nothing I could do. According to my theory, I just had to sit back and wait patiently until one or more of the stocks I had been stopped out of, or any other stocks I was watching, went towards a new higher box.

Eager and anxious, I watched from the sidelines with not a dollar invested, while prices continued to drop.

But no opportunity seemed to appear. What I did not know was that we were at the end of one phase of the great bull market. It was several months before this became evident and it was declared a bear market. Half the Wall Street analysts still discuss it. They say it was merely an intermediate reaction —a temporary halt in the rising market. They all agree, however, that prices collapsed.

Of course all these opinions are expressed by hindsight— when it is too late. The advice to get out of the market was not available when one needed it.

I recall the case of Hitler when he decided to invade Stalingrad. To him it was just another Russian town to be conquered and occupied. Nobody knew while the battle of Stalingrad was being fought that it was the turning point in the war. For a very long time, few people realized it.

Even when the German armies were halfway back, it was still talked about as strategic withdrawal. It was, in fact, the end of Hitler. The Nazi war bull market ended the day Hitler attacked Stalingrad.

In the same way, I realized that it was impossible for me to assess great historical turning points in the market when they began to happen. What fascinated me, as Wall Street prices continued to fall, was the gradual realization that my system of ducking out quickly with my stop-losses made such an assessment unnecessary.

I made the joyful discovery that my method had worked much better than I had dreamed. It had automatically released me well before the bad times came. The market had changed - but I was already out of it.

The most important aspect to me was that I had absolutely no hint whatsoever that the market would slide. How could I have had any information? I was too far away all the time. I had listened to no predictions, studied no fundamentals, and heard no rumors. I had simply gotten out on the basis of the behavior of my stocks.

Later when I studied the stocks I had sold automatically, I found that they subsequently slid down very low indeed in the recession period.

Look at the following table:

	1957 I sold at	1958 Lowest price	1958 Highest price
BALTIMORE & OHIO	55	22⅝	45¼
DAYSTROM	42¼	30	39¾
FOSTER WHEELER	59½	25⅛	39⅛
AEROQUIP	27½	16⅞	25¾
ALLIED CONTROL	48¼	33½	46½
DRESSER INDUSTRIES	54½	33	46⅝
JOY MANUFACTURING	68	38	54½
ALLEGHENY LUDLUM	56½	30⅛	49⅜

When I looked at this table, I thought this: If my stop-losses had not taken me out of the market I could have lost about 50% of my investment. I would have been like a man in a cage, locked in with my holdings and missing my opportunity to make a fortune. The only way I could have escaped would have been by smashing out, taking a 50% loss, possibly ruining myself, and gravely impairing my confidence for future deals.

I could, of course, have bought these stocks and "put them away.'* This is a classic solution among people who call themselves conservative investors. But by now I regarded them as pure gamblers. How can they be non-gamblers when they stay with a stock even if it continues to drop? A non-gambler must get out when his stocks fall. They stay in with the gambler's eternal hope of the turn of a lucky card.

I thought of the people who paid 250 for NEW YORK CENTRAL in 1929. If they were still holding it today it was worth about 27. Yet they would be indignant if you called them gamblers!

It was in this mood of non-gambling that I received my monthly statement in the first week of September 1957, and I began to check up on my accounts. I found I had made up the money I had lost on JONES & LAUGHLIN and my original capital of $37,000 was almost intact. Many of my operations had been moderately successful, but commissions and taxes had taken a great deal.

When I went into the accounts more closely I found I had the unenviable distinction of coming out of the greatest bull market in history with a lot of experience, a great amount of knowledge, much more confidence—and a net loss of $889.

THE TECHNO-FUNDAMENTALIST

CHAPTER 6

During the Baby-Bear Market

After a few weeks of being without a single share I decided to take a closer clinical look at the situation. To understand it clearly I made a comparison between the two markets.

The bull market I saw as a sunny summer camp filled with powerful athletes. But I had to remember that some stocks were stronger than others. The bear market? The summer camp had changed to a hospital. The great majority of stocks were sick— but some were more sick than others.

When the break came almost all of the stocks had been hurt or fractured. It was now a question of estimating how sick the stocks were and how long their sickness would last.

I reasoned that if a stock has fallen from 100 to 40, it will almost certainly not climb up to the same high again for a long, long time. It was like an athlete with a badly injured leg who would need a long period of recuperation before he could run and jump again as before. There was no doubt in my mind now that I could not make money by buying a stock and then trying to cheer it on. JONES & LAUGHLIN had convinced me of that. I could remember how I almost felt myself willing and pushing that stock upwards. It was a very human feeling, but it had no effect upon its market any more than spectators have on a horse race. If one horse is going to win, it will win, even if thousands of onlookers are cheering for another one.

It was the same now. I knew that if I bought a stock and turned out to be wrong, all the cheering and pushing in the world would not alter the price half a point. And there was no telling how far the market might fall. I did not like the trend, but I knew it was no use trying to fight it.

The situation reminded me of George Bernard Shaw's remark at the opening night of one of his plays. After the curtain fell everyone cheered and clapped except one man who booed. G.B.S. went up to him and said: "Don't you like my play?"

The man replied, "No, I don't." Whereupon Shaw said: "Neither do I, but what can the two of us do against all that crowd?"

So I accepted everything for what it was—not what I wanted it to be. I just stayed on the sidelines and waited for better times to come.

I firmly refused to trade—so emphatically that my broker wrote to me and asked the reason. I tried to explain it by making a joke: "This is a market for the birds. I see no reason why I should be in a bird- market."

The period that followed I spent like a runner limbering up for the race. Week after week, while I did not have any stock and the market was in a steady downtrend, I followed the quotations in Barron's. I tried to detect those stocks that resisted the decline. I reasoned that if they could swim against the stream, they were the ones that would advance most rapidly when the current changed.

After a while, when the first initial break in the market wore off, my opportunity came. Certain stocks began to resist the downward trend. They still fell, but while the majority dropped easily, following the mood of the general market, these stocks gave ground grudgingly. I could almost feel their reluctance.

On closer examination, I found the majority of these were companies whose earning trends pointed sharply upward. The conclusion was obvious: capital was flowing into these stocks, even in a bad market. This capital was following earning improvements as a dog follows a scent. This discovery opened my eyes to a completely new perspective.

I saw that it is true that stocks are the slaves of earning power. Consequently, I decided that while there may be many reasons behind any stock movement, I would look only for one: improving earning power or anticipation of it. To do that, I would marry my technical approach to the fundamental one. I would select stocks on their technical action in the market, but I would only buy them when I could give improving earning power as my fundamental reason for doing so.

This was how I arrived at my *techno-fundamentalis* theory, which I am still using today.

As to the practical application, I decided to take a 20-year view. That did not mean I wanted to hold a stock for 20 years. Nothing was more contrary to my intentions. But I looked out for those stocks, which were tied up with the future and where I could expect that revolutionary new products would sharply improve the company's earnings.

Certain industries were obvious at once, like electronics, missiles, rocket fuels. They were rapidly expanding, infant industries and, unless something unforeseen happened, their expansion should soon be reflected in the market. From my research into the history of the stock market, I knew that the basic principles governing stocks-of-the-future have always held good in Wall Street. In the years before automobiles, the smart operators went into railroads because they knew these would supersede the covered wagon and the stagecoach. A generation or so later, the shrewd investors moved out of railroads into automobiles. Forward-looking, expanding companies like GENERAL MOTORS and CHRYSLER were comparatively small firms then. But they represented the future. People who bought into them at that time and stayed with them during their expansion period made a lot of money. Now these are well-established stocks. They are not for the forward-looking speculator.

It is the same today, I reasoned. On the general theory of the buoyant future, stocks, which promise dynamic future development, should behave better than others. A sound stock, which is in tune with the jet age, might be worth 20 times as much in 20 years.

I knew that in this kind of stock there were definite fashions just as there are in women's clothes, and if I wanted to be successful it was important to search for fashionable stocks.

Women's fashions alter, and so do fashions in stocks. Women will raise or lower their hemlines one or two inches roughly every two or three years.

The same with stocks. While the fashion persists, the forward-looking investors get in and stay in. Then slowly the fashion fades and they are out. They are putting their money into a new-style stock. I knew I must watch eagerly for these fashion changes, or I might be left still holding a long-skirt stock when the new stocks were showing their knees. I might also miss, unless I was very alert, something sensationally new like the big-bosom era.

This is not so fanciful as it may seem. Take a mythical product like an automobile, which can also fly. Everybody is rushing for that company's stock. Yet in a converted stable in Oregon two men are working on an invention, which will far outclass the flying car.

Once that is ready for the market, and a company has been formed to handle it, the original flying car will be superseded. Its stock will start to slide. It will become old-fashioned.

This is an over-simplification and does not solve the problem: How to buy into this year's fashion? I could only do it by carefully watching the market for signs. If the fashion seemed to be moving away from the long skirt, there must be some other about-to-be-fashionable stock ready to take its place. What I had to do was to find stocks that would be hoisted up because they stirred people's imagination for the future.

On the basis of this thinking, I carefully watched stock-market quotations in this general bracket of expanding stocks in tune with the jet age. I was not interested in the company's individual products, whether it was metals for rockets, solid fuel, or advanced electronic equipment. In fact, I did not want to know what they made—that information might only inhibit me. I did not care what the company's products were, any more than I was influenced by the fact that the board chairman had a beautiful wife. But I did want to know whether the company belonged to a new vigorous infant industry and whether it behaved in the market according to my requirements.

This, of course, was directly against the advice of many financial writers with conservative backgrounds who have been pounding into investors for generations that they must study company reports and balance sheets, find out all they can about a stock's background, in order to make a wise investment.

I decided that was not for me. All a company report and balance sheet can tell you is the past and the present. They cannot tell the future. And it was for this I had to project my plans. I also humbly realized that that was only my attitude. I was looking for capital gain. A widow looking for dividend income had to think otherwise.

As I flew around the world, I was constantly searching for stocks that would climb into the stratosphere because of the vision of their future. This attitude was a preparation for what I suppose you could call high-territory trading. I looked for stocks that I thought could make new highs and I decided to give them my full attention when they had climbed on to the launching pad and were preparing to rocket up. Now these stocks would be more expensive than ever before and so they would look too dear to the uninitiated. But they could become dearer. I made up my mind to buy high and sell higher.

Using my hard-bought training, I diligently attempted to find these expensive-but-cheap, high-velocity stocks. I searched constantly for them because I felt sure that they would move up at the first sign of a better market.

I carefully watched a dozen stocks, which seemed to be in this category, checking their quotations every week, analyzing their behavior for any sign of a hardening.

I closely observed their price action, and I was on the alert for any unusual activity as well. I had not forgotten the importance of volume.

I also prepared myself to operate in higher-priced stocks. This was because of the brokerage commissions. When I examined the rates I discovered that it was cheaper to invest $10,000 in a $100 stock than in a $10 stock. Here is why:

Let us suppose I wanted to invest my $10,000 in one stock. I could do it in several ways.

For instance I could buy:

1000 shares of $10 stock
or

500 shares or $20 stock
or

100 shares of $100 stock

The New York Stock Exchange commission rates were:

Price of Stock	Commission per 100 shares
$ 1	$ 6
$ 5	$10
$10	$15
$20	$25
$30	$30

$40	$35
$50	$40
$100	$45

To invest my $10,000 would cost me (buying plus selling):

In the case of the $1 0 stock	$300.
In the case of the $20 stock	$250.
In the case of the $100 stock	$ 90.

If my buying point was correct, the broker's commission was not important. It came off my profit. But, if my timing was wrong and I was stopped out—that was another matter. Then the two commissions, one for buying and one for selling, had to be added to my loss. So as you see, my mistakes would be much less costly if I bought higher- priced stocks.

As I watched the market continually sinking, I knew that it could not sink forever. Sooner or later stocks would begin to move upwards. They always had. Bear markets were always followed by bull markets. The educated art was to watch for the first signs, be sure they were real, and buy in before everyone else noticed and the prices began to rise too high.

My mind went back to the battle of Waterloo. At this famous battle Rothschild had an agent who, as soon as victory was certain, set off for London and informed Rothschild. Rothschild started buying every British government share he could before anyone else heard the news. When they did, of course, the shares rocketed and Rothschild sold at a huge profit. The principle remains the same in Wall Street today. Communications are much quicker but the ancient art remains the same - to get in faster than the other fellow.

That was the position for which I had now trained myself for five years. I knew I had learned an enormous amount. My Canadian period taught me not to gamble; my fundamentalist period taught me about industry groups and their earning trends; my technical period taught me how to interpret price-action and the technical position of stocks - and now I reinforced myself by piecing them all together. It was like the solution of an intriguing jigsaw puzzle where finally all the pieces fall beautifully into place. I was certain this method would prove successful in the future. I felt calm and confident waiting for the market-tide to turn.

After a few months, what I was waiting for began to happen. Reading *Barton's,* I noticed that, while the averages were still showing a decline as they had for several months, a few stocks were beginning to peep up, almost as unnoticeable as primrose buds on a winter's day. It was still a question whether these tender shoots would survive or be killed by frost. But when I noticed this slow awakening, I began to sense the end of this baby-bear market—at least for certain stocks.

I did suspect one thing, however—and that was that the leaders in the previous market would probably not lead again. I felt sure they had fulfilled their place in history and they would not—for the time being—reach the same dizzy heights that had brought so much money to the investors who had followed them.

I had to find new ones. Later this was proved right because hidden away in the market quotes during this period were some stocks which were apparently of not much interest to anybody. At that time— November 1957—they were certainly of no interest to me. I had hardly heard of them.

They were:

UNIVERSAL PRODUCTS	quoted at	20
THIOKOL CHEMICAL	quoted at	64
TEXAS INSTRUMENTS	quoted at	23
ZENITH RADIO	quoted at	116
FAIRCHILD CAMERA	quoted at	19

These stocks were not dead. They were only sleeping the promising sleep of the unborn. One day soon they were destined to wake up. They were going to leap into a new leadership of the market. They were going to make me $2,000,000.

Chapter 7

The Theory Starts to Work

While most Wall Street stocks drifted or dropped, I continued my dancing tour of the world. In November 1957 I was appearing at the "Arc En Ciel" in Saigon when I noticed in Barron's a stock unknown to me called LORILLARD.

I did not know then that they were the manufacturers of a particular brand of filter-tip cigarettes and the filter-tip craze was about to sweep America, causing their production to leap up astronomically. Out in Saigon, all I knew was that LORILLARD began to emerge from the swamp of sinking stocks like a beacon. In spite of the bad market, it rose from 17 until, in the first week of October; it esta blished itself in the narrow box 24/27. Its volume for that week was 126,700 shares, which sharply contrasted with its usual 10,000 shares earlier in the year.

The steady rise in price and the high volume indicated to me that there was a tremendous interest in this stock. As for its fundamentals, I was satisfied as soon as I found out about the wide acceptance of their "Kent" and "Old Gold" cigarettes. I decided that if it showed signs of going above 27 I would buy it.

I asked my broker to cable me daily quotes. It soon became clear from these quotes that certain knowledgeable people were trying to get into this stock in spite of the general state of the market. Few people at that time had the faintest indication that LORILLARD was to make Wall Street history, that it was to shoot up to a most astounding high in a relatively short time, watched by the amazed and gasping financial community.

We were at the depth of the baby-bear market and the atmosphere was rather gloomy. But, as if unperturbed by the general pessimism, LORILLARD was happily jumping up and down in its little cage.

By mid-November 1957 it became even more independent and it began to push upward toward what I estimated would be a 27/32 box. This isolated strength in the face of general weakness was very impressive to me. I felt I had sufficient proof of its strength, and I decided to become a bull in a bear market. I sent the following cable from Bangkok:

"BUY 200 LORILLARD 27½ ON STOP WITH 26 STOPLOSS"

As you see, although I felt quite secure in my judgment with my merged technical and fundamental viewpoints, I did not for one moment consider abandoning my chief defensive weapon—the stop-loss order. No matter how well built your house is, you would not think of forgetting to insure it against fire.

Within a few days, I received confirmation that I had bought 200 LORILLARD at 27½. I was well satisfied with my purchase, and braced myself for a big rise.

This came, but not the way I had assessed it. My first experience was disheartening. On Tuesday, November 26th, the stock dropped back exactly to my stop-loss of 26 and I was sold out. To add insult to injury, seconds after I was stopped out, it started to rise and closed at 26¾.

However, the reaction was so short and the rise that followed so firm, that I decided to go back into it. That same week I bought back my shares at 28¾. Again I fixed my stop-loss at 26.

But this time, LORILLARD'S behavior was perfect. As the days went by, I was satisfied to see that the quotations never came close to my stop - loss. This was a firm indication that I was on the right track, and that my theory applied to this stock.

I happened to be right. In December 1957, LORILLARD rose over 30 and made a new 31/55 box. My experiences with similar stock movements in the past told me that it was being accumulated. I felt I had the right stock. Now it was a question of getting into it with more money at the right time.

I carefully watched my daily quotes. I looked for the right moment as a fighter looks for an opening to land his blow. Towards the end of January, after a false move, the big surge-through which I had been expecting occurred, LORILLARD started to move decisively out of its box.

This seemed to be the ideal moment. Everything was encouraging – the technical action, the fundamentals, the pattern. Also, the New York Stock Exchange had just lowered its margin requirements from 70% to 50%. This meant that my limited capital now had much more purchasing power. Every $1,000 could buy $2,000 worth of stock. This was important to me, because I needed my funds for another stock I was watching at that time.

I was flying from Bangkok to Japan. It was from there I sent out my cables to add a further 400 shares to my holdings. These were bought for me at 35 and 36½.

In the weeks that followed, the stock's behavior continued to be exemplary. It was exciting to watch my theory being vindicated in practice. While I was traveling around the world dancing, LORILLARD was steadily dancing about in its box. It would do this for a short time and then, with an impeccable, almost predictable thrust, move into the box above, LORILLARD boxes began piling on top of each other like a beautifully constructed pyramid. I watched them fascinated. I had never seen a stock behave so perfectly as this. It was acting as though my theory had been built around it.

On February 17, 1958, LORILLARD bounced up to 44⅜. I was feeling very pleased with myself and the stock when, two days later, I received a cable in Tokyo which frightened me.

In one single day my stock had dropped to a low of 36¾ and closed at 37¾.

I was baffled. This move was completely unexpected. I did not know how to explain it. I rapidly cabled New York and raised my stop-loss to 36, less than 2 points below the day's closing price. I felt if it dropped there, I would be sold out and still make a nice profit on my first purchase.

As I was in Tokyo, I could not know the Wall Street rumors which had driven the stock down that day. All I knew was that it acted badly. Later I found out there had been a report saying that filter-tips were not so efficacious against lung cancer as they were claimed to be and this had panicked a lot of people out of the stock.

Fortunately, the setback was very short, and my stop-loss was not touched off. This convinced me of the stock's power and I decided to buy an additional 400 shares. I paid 38⅝.

Almost immediately we left this price behind. The quotes came in: 39¾-40¼-42.

I was very happy. I felt as if I had become a partner in an immense new development. Everything looked as if I had planned it.

It was at this time that I received from my broker three weeks' issues of a well-known advisory service. Week after week this service strongly urged its subscribers to sell LORILLARD short. The third recommendation read like this:

"Lorillard was obviously under distribution around 44 last week after we told you to start it on the short side."

This amazed me, but I had long ago become so disillusioned with advisory services that I did not pay attention to it.

Instead I started to recommend LORILLARD to any American tourist who mentioned stock market to me. I was genuinely trying to be helpful. My enthusiasm is best illustrated by what happened one day in the Erawan Hotel in Bangkok. One afternoon at lunch

I was introduced to the president of one of the largest American shipping companies. During our conversation he mentioned that his holdings in the stock market amounted to $3,000,000. They were broken up in the following way:

$2,500,000 worth of STANDARD OIL (NEW JERSEY) $500,000 worth of LORILLARD.

"What do you think about it?" he asked. What did I think of it? He could not have asked a better man.

I immediately told him to sell all his holdings in JERSEY STANDARD and switch his funds into LORILLARD. That was what I would have done.

A year later I met him at a party in New York, LORILLARD was then above 80.

"What's your latest stock market advice?" he asked me.

"Advice?" I said. I was astonished. "Wasn't that $3,000,000 worth of advice I gave you in Bangkok enough?"

"It would have been," he said. "If I had followed it." In the third week of March 1958, LORILLARD entered on an even more definite upward- thrust. It jumped 4 1/8 points in one week, its volume increased to an astounding 316,600 and it established itself decisively in the 50/54 box.

In the second week of April LORILLARD left its new box. It pushed through to a new high of 55¼ but immediately dropped back to its former 50/54 box. As I did not contemplate a further purchase this did not upset me unduly. However, I cautiously raised my stop-loss to 49.

I also wavered for a moment, on the verge of selling, but I decided against it. By now I had trained myself to be patient and, although I could have taken an easy $20 per share profit on my earliest purchase, I sat back determined not to take too quick a profit.

My cost figures for LORILLARD were:

200 shares at 28¾	$5,808.76
200 shares at 35	$7,065.00
200 shares at 36½	$7,366.50
400 shares at 38⅝	$15,587.24
Total 1,000 shares	$3 5,827.50

I carried the last three purchases on 50% margin. This enabled me to keep the rest of my capital for a further investment, which turned out to be a stock called DINERS' CLUB. I first became interested in this stock at the turn of the year, while I still battled with LORILLARD.

DINERS' CLUB had just split 2-for-l, and in the last week of January 1958 its weekly volume swelled to 23,400, which I considered unusually high for this stock.

As this increase in volume was accompanied by an advance in price, I decided to check the stock's fundamentals. They were reassuring. The company was a near-monopoly in an expanding field. The credit- card system, of which it was one of the pioneers, was firmly established. The company's earnings were in a definite upward trend. With these factors in mind, I bought 500 shares at 24½. My stop-loss was 21 ⅝

Now the question was which direction the stock would take. My first LORILLARD purchase had already shown me a profit, and I reasoned that if it came to the worst, I would lose it on DINERS' CLUB. But I did not. A few days after my purchase, the stock began to advance.

According to my theory, I immediately bought another 500 shares—at 26 1/8. On both buys, I took advantage of the new 50% marein.

The pattern evolved perfectly—first a 28/30, then a 32/36 box. The last penetration was accompanied by a volume of 52,600 shares for the week. This was higher than any other week's volume in the newly- split stock's history.

As I saw my profits piling up, I did not for a moment forget to trail my stop-loss insurance behind the rise. First I raised it to 27, then to 31.

In the fourth week of March the stock penetrated a new 36½/40 box and seemed to establish itself there. I summed up my position in DINERS' CLUB. I had brought:

500 shares at 24½	$12,353.15
500 shares at 26⅛	13,167.65
Total 1,000 shares	$25,520.80

I already had a profit of more than $10,000. Still, according to my theory, I had to hold on. The stock behaved as if it would go even higher. Every indication pointed to that.

But suddenly, unexpectedly, my cables began to read differently. It was difficult to understand why, but I began to feel uncomfortable. The stock seemed to have lost its will to rise. It looked as though its last pyramid would hesitate on the brink of going into reverse. It almost seemed ready to tumble. So as not to get caught in any collapse, I decided to raise my stop-loss to the unusually narrow margin of 36⅜.

In the fourth week of April, the event against which I had insured myself occurred, DINERS' CLUB broke through the lower limit of its box and I was sold out. I received $35,848.85. I had made an overall profit of $10,328.05.

For the first time—as I sat in my room in the Imperial Hotel in Tokyo with the cable in my hand, which said I had made $10,000 profit—I felt all my study and worry over the past few years had been worth it. I was beginning to come out on top.

Six weeks later I received news, which in some ways made me feel more elated than the $10,000, because it completely confirmed the technical side of my approach. It was officially announced that American Express had decided to launch a rival to Diners' Club. This had been the reason for the hesitation of the stock near the 36 mark. Some people had known this before the announcement and were selling out. Without knowing about it, I was their partner.

Being in the Far East, I could not possibly know of any rival organization being set up. Yet the technical side of my system based on the price action had warned me to get out.

During all the time that I spent with LORIIXARD and DINERS' CLUB, I never neglected to follow the quotations of other stocks in Barron's. This began to show me that there was a great interest springing up in a stock called E. L. BRUCE, a small Memphis firm. The stock was quoted on the American Stock Exchange. On closer examination, I learned that the company made hardwood flooring. This most certainly did not fit my fundamental requirements, but the technical pattern was so compelling that I could not take my eyes off it.

What amazed me was the movement of E. L. BRUCE on Street. It usually traded below 5,000 shares a week. Then it suddenly woke up and started to move. In the second week of April 1958, its volume rose to an astonishing 19,100 shares. Thereafter the weekly volume climbed to 41,500–54,200–76,500 shares, with the price jumping 5 to 8 points weekly without any sign of downward reaction.

BRUCE went from 18 in February to 50 at the beginning of May. Only then came its first reaction, which carried it back to 43J4. I could not be sure, of course, but this reaction seemed to me only a temporary halt, a refueling. I felt it would continue to rise. I tried to find a fundamental reason, but I could not. Still, the volume was there, the price action was there, the rhythm of the advance was there.

I began to feel like a man sitting in a darkened theatre, waiting for the curtain to go up on a thriller. As I flew from Tokyo to Calcutta, I puzzled over the BRUCE quotations every hour of the way. It had a wider, freer range than most stocks, and I could not place a definite frame around it. Flying over the Indian Ocean, I made up my mind to make an exception. Fundamentals or no fundamentals, if it went over 50, I would buy it, and I would buy a lot of it.

But I needed money. My DINERS' CLUB sale had released some of my funds, but that was not enough. I could have used my savings, but after the JONES & LAUGHLIN disaster I had decided never again to risk more money than I could afford to lose without ruining myself. Consequently I have never again added to my market funds from my show-business income.

The only possible thing to do was to take a close look at my old friend LORILLARD. Was it still behaving well?

It was not. Its penetrations were not decisive, its reactions were deeper. I decided to take my money out of LORILLARD and be ready to invest it in BRUCE. I sold my 1,000 shares the second week in May for an average price of 57⅜. The total price on the sale was $56,880.45. My profit on the deal was $21,052.95.

This, with the $10,000 I had made from DINERS' CLUB, meant that in five months I had nearly doubled my capital. I felt pleased and proud and ready, like a giant-killer, to deal with a powerful and erratic stock like BRUCE.

I made special preparation for this fight. I had concluded after the LORILLARD deal that my system was working so well that I did not want to entrust it into the hands of one firm. I felt if anyone were to follow my operations, this might make it difficult for me. I called New York and opened accounts with two other brokerage firms.

In the third week of May 1958, I cabled New York to buy 500 BRUCE at 50¾ with my automatic on-stop buy order. I put in a stop-loss of 48.

In the following days the stock acted so beautifully that I decided to take full advantage of the existing 50% margin conditions. When

I saw that my stop-loss was not touched off I proceeded with further purchases, each of which was protected by stop-losses between 47 and 48. I figured that, should I be stopped out, I would only lose my DINERS' CLUB profit.

These are the details of my purchases:

500 shares at 50¾	$25,510.95
500 shares at 51⅛	25,698.90
500 shares at 51¾	26,012.20
500 shares at 52¾	26,513.45
500 shares at 53⅝	26,952.05
Total 2,500 shares	$130,687.55

My timing was right, E. L. BRUCE really began to climb as if drawn upwards by a magnet. As I watched it, I became amazed at the way it soared. It was spectacular.

I just sat in Calcutta gazing at my daily quotes. Soon they told me the stock had surged over 60. After a slight hesitation, it suddenly broke out again. By June 13th, it had advanced to 77.

It was obvious even in faraway India that something fantastic was happening on the American Stock Exchange. I had to fight a hard battle with myself not to phone New York and find out what was going on. No, I said to myself as I felt like calling my brokers, that will only mean rumors and you may do something silly.

No man's resolution and patience were more severely tested than mine as I sat in the Grand Hotel at Calcutta, wondering what Wall Street was doing.

A few days later my nail-gnawing impatience was changed to terror by a call from New York. It was one of my brokers, and he nearly stopped my heartbeat. He said: "They have suspended trading in BRUCE on the American Stock Exchange." I nearly dropped the phone as I listened. I was terrified. Stopped trading in BRUCE stock! I had over $60,000, my entire capital, invested in it.

Did this mean I had lost my money? It was with some difficulty that I was able to concentrate enough to listen. It was minutes before I recovered enough to hear what he had to say.

With my emotions running amok, it took me a long time to understand that far from being broke, I now could sell BRUCE for $100 a share in the over-the-counter market. I was completely confused. $100 a share! What was this?

I was trembling while he told me the story over the telephone from New York to Calcutta.

Certain traders on Wall Street, basing their views on a purely fundamental approach, had decided that BRUCE'S book value and earnings indicated that the stock's price should not be more than $30 a share. Therefore, they had started to sell the stock short between 45 and 50, confident they would be able to fulfill their bargains by buying it back at a price much nearer 30.

They made a grave mistake, because there was one factor they did not know about. A New York manufacturer named Edward Gilbert was trying to oust the Bruce family from control of the company. He and his associates were trying to obtain a majority of the 314,600 shares outstanding which the Bruce family owned. It was this move that had rocketed the price. The volume was terrific, and more than 275,000 Bruce shares were traded during a period of ten weeks.

The short-sellers who had so misjudged the market jostled each other to push the stock to dizzy heights in their frantic efforts to buy it. They were caught with their pants down by the mysterious upward surge of the stock and they could not buy the shares at any price to fulfill their obligations.

Finally, as it was impossible to assure an orderly market because of the frenzied dealings, the American Stock Exchange suspended trading. But this made no difference to the desperate short sellers. They still had to deliver the stock. Now they were willing to pay anything over-the- counter for BRUCE.

I listened in a daze to all this. My broker asked me whether, since the over-the-counter price per share was now 100, I would instruct him to sell at this price.

I thought back to my daily cables, and how they had begun to paint an amazing picture of BRUCE to me. I remembered the ordeal I had undergone as I steeled myself not to telephone to find out what was happening because this would come under the heading of "rumors" which I had sworn never to listen to again. I recalled how I held on while my daily quotes revealed to me BRUCE'S sensational upward progress, and I did not know what to do.

Should I still hold on? I was faced with a very hard decision. I was offered a big, tempting profit. As I listened to my broker, I felt strongly urged to sell the stock. After all, selling at 100 meant I would make a fortune.

I thought hard while I listened. Then I made one of the most momentous decisions of my life. I said: "No, I will not sell at 100. I have no reason to sell an advancing stock. I will hold onto it."

I did. It was a big decision and a difficult one, but it proved exactly right. Several times within the next few weeks I received urgent telephone calls reporting higher and higher offers for my shares from brokers in various parts of the United States. I gradually sold out the stock on the over-the-counter market in blocks of 100 and 200 shares— for an average price of 171.

This was my first really big killing in the market. I made $295,305.45 profit on this operation.

This was a tremendous event for me. I was so happy I did not know which way to turn. I told my story to everyone who cared to listen. I showed my telegrams to them. The only reaction was: "Who gave you the tip?" I tried to explain that no one had given me a tip, that I had done it all by myself and that I was so happy and excited exactly for that reason.

Nobody believed me. I am sure that every one of my friends in

Calcutta still believes today that Mr. Gilbert himself had taken me into his confidence.

Chapter 8

My First Half-Million

The overwhelming success of my handling of E. L. BRUCE should have made me more eager and less cautious. Yet, somehow it made me more cautious. I had made over $325,000 in nine months' investment, and I was determined not to lose it by a wrong move. So many operators have made big money in nine months and lost it in nine weeks. I decided this would not happen to me. The first step I took was to withdraw half of my profits from the market. With my remaining capital I eyed the market warily, watching for possible new well- behaved stocks. As so often after a coup, I had very little success for a month or two immediately afterwards.

I cautiously bought 500 shares of MOLYBDENUM. I bought it at 27, paying $13,606.25. Almost immediately, I was stopped out at 26½, so that I got back $13,123.78.

I had a go at HAVEG INDUSTRIES. I bought 500 shares at 31⅜, paying $15,860.95. It turned around and looked as if it was going to slip under 30, so I sold out at 30½ for $15,056.94.

Then, as I saw nothing interesting, I ventured back to LORILLARD. This stock, which had once stood out in the bear market like a tree in a desert, had now become a rather weary, slow-moving elderly gentleman. But I suppose I had a sentimental attachment towards it because it had done so well for me the first time. For a long time I could not leave it alone. It became my American "pet." This was an utterly wrong attitude but I could not seem to help it.

Three times I bought into it, because I thought it was climbing towards a higher box. Three times I sold out because the new box did not materialize.

This is how the LORILLARD operation looked:

1,000 shares

Bought at	70l/2	($70,960.50)	
Sold at	677/8	($67,369.74)	
			Loss $3,590.76

500 shares

Bought at	69 1/8	($34,792.05)	
Sold at	67¾	($33,622.42)	
			Loss $1,169.63

1,000 shares

Bought at	67¾	($68,207.80)	
Sold at	67	($66,495.66)	
			Loss $1,712.14

That did it. The third loss finally broke my sentimental attachment and I did not buy in again. I realized that as LORILLARD now moved at a very leisurely pace, it was obviously no longer a stock for me.

After I withdrew from LORILLARD, I sat back and assessed my overall position.

It looked like this:

	Profit	Losses
LORILLARD	$21,052.95	$6,472.53
DINERS' CLUB	10,328.05	
E. L. BRUCE	295,305.45	
MOLYBDENUM		482.47
HAVEG		804.01
INDUSTRIES		
	$326,686.45	$7,759.01

My overall profit was $318,927.44.

During the time I was getting in and out of LORILLARD, I was continuously looking for stocks that would fit my theory. One very important factor that urged me to deeper search was that the general market started to get stronger. As I felt this strength becoming pronounced, I wanted to take full advantage of it by getting into a promising stock as early as possible.

Among the stocks that caught my eye was a little, unknown company called UNIVERSAL PRODUCTS. It was quoted around 35, running up and down between 3 5 ⅞ and 33½ I found out it was an electronics company and therefore I felt it qualified as far as my techno- fundamentalist theory was concerned.

In July 1958, when I was still in Calcutta, I asked New York for daily quotes. The story they told me was very promising. However, my recent LORILLARD losses reminded me that I could be wrong several times in a row and I wanted to act very cautiously. I thought I could get a better feel of the stock's movement if I actually owned some of it, so I decided to make a pilot buy. I sent out the following cable:

"BUY 300 UNIVERSAL PRODUCTS 35¼ OR BETTER"

Next day, when I received the advice that 300 shares of UNIVERSAL PRODUCTS had been bought for me at 35¼, I wired:

"ENTER STOPLOSS 32½"

Now there was nothing to do but sit back, watch and wait for the next move.

At this period, I was flying back and forth across India rather frequently. But cable quotes on UNIVERSAL PRODUCTS followed me everywhere. In the third week of August 1958, I was in Srinagar in Kashmir, when I noticed that the stock was beginning to firm up. I cabled:

"BUY 1200 UNIVERSAL PRODUCTS 36½ ON STOP 33 STOPLOSS"

When I returned to the Imperial Hotel in New Delhi I received the notice: "BROUGHT 1200 U 36½ ON STOP U 36¾ (37⅞ - 35⅜) ETC"

This meant I had bought my stock at 36½ and it closed at 36¾. While it did not decisively pull away from my buying price, it closed above it. Now the question was: Will my stock continue to advance or will it return to its former box?

I was quite excited. Although I had already fixed the limit of my possible eventual loss, now it was a question of whether my judgment was right or wrong. I could hardly wait for next day's cable. When it finally arrived, it showed that UNIVERSAL PRODUCTS had closed at 38 1/8. Its range for the day was 38¾-37½. This meant I was right—at least for the time being.

In the next few days the stock continued to advance, and when I was in Karachi I bought another 1,500 shares at 40. Shortly thereafter, UNIVERSAL PRODUCTS changed its name to UNIVERSAL CONTROLS and split 2-for-l. It continued to act well but after my last purchase I decided that I had as much UNIVERSAL CONTROLS as I cared to carry.

This was my exact position: (The prices in this table, and all following tables, are average.)

Pilot buy of 300 at 3 5 ¼	$10,644.93
1,200 at 36J4	44,083.56
1,500 at 40	60,585.00
Total 3,000 shares	$115,313.49

This gave me 6,000 shares of the newly split stock. Now I sat back and held on while the stock started to skyrocket.

At the beginning of December, when I saw that UNIVERSAL CONTROLS was behaving correctly, I recommended the stock to my secretary. I told him to buy it at 31¾. I said: "If it goes below 30 take a loss and sell it, otherwise hold it for a big rise. If you have to take a loss I will cover it."

It so happened that his father was an old-fashioned, pure fundamentalist and when he heard what I had suggested, he told his son not to be such a fool. His argument was: What was the point of buying a stock if it might go down? He reckoned you should only buy stock that was sure to rise—as if anyone could be sure. He also said he wanted to examine the books of the company to see if it was in good condition.

My secretary took his father's advice. He did not invest any money, but waited while the old man was carefully examining the books. While he was engrossed in this task the stock went up to 50.

Simultaneously with UNIVERSAL CONTROLS, I was watching another stock whose action was fascinating to me. It was THIOKOL CHEMICAL.

It first attracted my attention in February 1958, when I was in Tokyo. It had just split 2-for-l and was the object of heavy trading before it quieted down into a 39/47 box. It stayed calmly in this area for several months.

As I regularly checked it in Barron's, this area of tranquility looked like a pond on a summer's day. But somehow I had the feeling it was a calm that precedes the storm.

In March I cabled New York:

"QUOTE THIOKOL"

The quotes duly arrived but, except for a few weeks of short-lived flurry in April, nothing noteworthy happened. After a few weeks I sent the following cable from Hong Kong:

“STOP THIOKOL QUOTES START QUOTING AGAIN IF RISES OVER 45”

I reasoned that if it reached again toward the upper frame of its box that would be the moment to watch it again. It was in the first week of August that THIOKOL quotes started to reappear in my telegrams. Above 45 it looked as though it was flexing its muscles for an upward jump. I decided for a pilot buy, and cabled:

"BUY 200 THIOKOL 47¼"

The order was executed at this price for a cost of $9,535.26.

After that it took three weeks for THIOKOL to find its true dynamics. At the end of August I felt the moment had come. I cabled New York:

"BUY 1300 THIOKOL 49½ ON STOP"

The purchase was executed at 49⅞ on September 2, 1958. The cost was $65,408.72.

With my 1,500 shares I saw the stock rapidly rising over 50 and trading in the range of 52-56.

A week later I receives notice from Thiokol had decided to issue stock- rights. These were given as bonuses to the holders of the stock at the rate of one right per share. In turn, with 12 of these rights you could buy one share of THIOKOL at the special price of $42. As the stock was quoted over 50, this was cheap indeed—if you wanted to exercise your stock-rights. If not, you could sell them on the American Stock Exchange where they were listed and traded for a limited period.

However, there was another important feature about these rights that made them very interesting. According to stock exchange rules, if the rights were being used to purchase the company's stock you could take advantage of what they called a "special subscription account." When you deposited your rights in this account, the broker was permitted to lend you up to 75% of the current market value of the stock. In addition, there was no commission charge on the purchase.

I jumped on this eagerly. Here was a unique opportunity for me to buy a great deal of stock on credit. I decided to plunge into this with all my free cash. I made a quick rough accounting of my position. Here is how I stood:

Original Investment	$ 36,000
Total Profits (after deducting loses)	319,000
Total Capital	$355,000
Cash Withdrawn	160,000
Free for Investment	$195,000
Purchases now Held	
3,000 UNIVERSAL PRODUCTS	$115,300
1,500 THIOKOL	75,000
	$190,300
70% cash under margin rules	$133,000
Free for further investment	$ 62,000

But now a curious situation developed. As I tried to make my arrangement with New York, I discovered that–in spite of the regulation permitting a 75% loan–there was wide disagreement among brokers concerning the amount that I could borrow from them in a special subscription account. While one broker was only willing to lend 75% of the purchase price of the stock, another was willing to advance a full 75% of the market value of the stock, THIOKOL being quoted around 55, the latter proposition was an extraordinarily attractive credit situation. I proceeded to take advantage of it.

I bought 36,000 rights at an average price of I 5/16 for which I paid $49,410. They entitled me to buy 3,000 THIOKOL at $42 per share. These cost me $126,000, but under the rights-subscription I only had to add another $6,000 cash. The rest of the money was loaned to me by one of my brokers.

This arrangement looked so favorable that I made up my mind to take further advantage of these unique credit conditions.

I figured out that by selling my original lot of 1,500 THIOKOL shares I could buy twice as much back under the special subscription rules.

I sold my stock at an average price of 53^2. This gave me a new buying power of $57,000. With this I bought a second block of 36,000 rights. Just as in the previous operation, I converted them into a second block of 3,000 shares of THIOKOL stock.

The operation looked like this:

(a) Sold 1,500 shares THIOKOL stock;

(b) Bought 36,000 THIOKOL rights, and with these

(c) Bought 3,000 shares THIOKOL stock.

My total cost for 6,000 shares was $350,820.

In the second week of December, THIOKOL shifted from the American to the New York Stock Exchange. It immediately moved up 8 points and the following week it was touching the 100 mark. As it continued its upward move, my broker must have become nervous, because I received a telegram, which said:

"YOUR THIOKOL PROFITS NOW $250,000"

This came to me while I was staying at the Georges V Hotel in Paris. I suddenly realized I had been so busy watching the quotes that I had almost forgotten about the paper profits piling up. Added to my profits in BRUCE, I now had a profit of over half-a-million dollars! This was much more money in fact than I ever thought I would own. It would make me a rich man for life.

The realization that I had all this money came to me with startling suddenness. Every fiber in my being seemed to be saying, "Sell, Sell." It was the biggest temptation in the world.

What should I do? Would the stock rise still higher—or should I take my profit and get out? Perhaps it wouldn't rise any higher—there might be a fallback. It was a terrible dilemma, the old one of "when to sell" much magnified because of the large amount of money at stake. If I did the right thing here, it would change my whole life. If I did the wrong thing, I would regret it forever.

I felt very alone. No one on earth could give me any advice on what to do in this situation. I decided to go out and have a few drinks by myself and consider the situation. Before I went out, I sat down at my dressing table and wrote on a little card, "Remember BRUCE!" I thought this would remind me of what I had learned in the past.

As I wandered around Paris, I kept fingering this little card in my pocket. Every time I felt like sending a cable to my brokers telling them to sell THIOKOL, I pulled out this card, looked at it and hesitated.

Finally, I decided not to sell. It was the best example of my new market technique and it was anything but easy to do. By the time I arrived back at my hotel I was exhausted. I must have looked more like a man about to commit suicide than one who had just made himself a small fortune.

But I was proved right, THIOKOL continued to rise and by making that decision in Paris, I was able to hold on and make much more money out of the stock.

A few weeks later, in January 1959, I returned to New York. When I landed at Idlewild Airport, I was holding 6,000 THIOKOL and 6,000 UNIVERSAL CONTROLS. They were both doing very well indeed, THIOKOL was standing on the 100 mark and UNIVERSAL CONTROLS had risen to 45.

In New York, my first appointment was to see my brokers and discuss my "Wall Street dealings with them. They told me that, according to their books, my investments had made me well over half a million dollars.

I felt elated, confident and successful. I booked myself a room at the Plaza Hotel and decided that during my stay I would continue my stock-market dealings from close quarters.

How little did I know I was preparing to make a complete fool of myself? Within the next few weeks I was to bring myself within whistling distance of ruin.

Chapter 9

My Second Crisis

The half-million-dollar news gave me enormous confidence. I had a very clear conception of how I had done it and I was also convinced I could repeat the feat again. I had no doubt that I had mastered my art. Working with my cables, I had developed a sort of sixth sense. I could "feel" my stocks. This was no different from the feeling that a musical expert develops. His ear will detect a flat note, which is inaudible to the ordinary listener.

I could almost tell what stocks would do. If after an eight-point advance a stock dropped back four points, I did not become alarmed. I expected it to do just that. If a stock started to firm up, I could often predict the day its advance would start. It was a mysterious, unexplainable instinct, but there was no question in my mind that I possessed it. This filled me with a tremendous sense of power.

It is therefore not the slightest bit surprising that I slowly started to imagine I was a Napoleon of finance. I felt I was about to march along a glittering road. I was not aware of any perils. I did not know that along the way a dangerous giant lay in wait. After all, I reasoned to myself rather smugly, how many people could do what I had done?

I decided to really get down to business. If I could make half a million, what was to stop me from making two, three or even five million? Although the margin requirement had recently been raised to 90 per cent, I was convinced that by using the $160,000 I had set aside from my BRUCE profits, I could lay the basis of a new fortune. I intended to start serious day-to-day dealings on the spot—dealings that would make my previous buying and selling seem like very small potatoes.

The truth was that as my pocket had strengthened, my head had weakened. I became over-confident, and that is the most dangerous state of mind anyone can develop in the stock market. It was not long before I received the bitter lesson the market always hands out to those who think they can carelessly master it.

After a few days in New York, I decided to establish closer contact with the market. Possessing what I thought was a foolproof system; I believed that if I moved nearer to the market, nothing could stop me from making a fortune each day. As the scene of my future triumphs, I chose the uptown office of one of my brokers.

I was fascinated by my first visit to the office. The boardroom was large, with chairs placed in front of an ever-moving little machine, the stock-ticker. The atmosphere was exciting, filled with electricity. The people in the room, like hangers-on in Monte Carlo, were nervous, exalted. There was an air of action, bustle, and noise. Tickers ticking, typewriters pounding, telegraph machines clacking, clerks busily rushing around. From every direction I heard sentences like: "GOODYEAR doesn't look good to me." "I am getting out of ANACONDA." "The market is ripe for a reaction."

The first day I was quite unperturbed by this taut, electric atmosphere. With my success behind me I felt I was above the anxieties, hopes and fears of these tense people. But this did not last long. As I began trading day to day from the boardroom, I gradually abandoned my detachment and started to join them. I opened my ears to the confusing combination of facts, opinions and gossip. I read the market letters. I also started to answer questions like, "What do you think of the market?" or "What do you know that's cheap?" All this had a deadly effect on me.

In a few days of trading, I threw overboard everything I had learned over the past six years. I did everything I had trained myself not to do. I talked to brokers. I listened to rumors. I was never off the ticker.

It was as if the "get-rich-quick" demon had gotten hold of me. I completely lost the clear perspective I had so carefully built up through my cables. Step by step I led myself along a path where I began to lose my skill.

The first thing that deserted me was my sixth sense. I did not "feel" anything. All I could see was a jungle of stocks running up and down without rhyme or reason. Then my independence went. I gradually abandoned my system and adopted the attitude of the others. The first thing I knew, I was following the crowd. My reason forsook me and emotion took over completely.

It is easier to understand how difficult it was for me to cling to my system if I explain it this way: Yell "fire" in a crowded theatre and what happens? People rush for the exit, killing, injuring each other. A drowning man will struggle, grasp his would-be rescuer and perhaps pull him under too. They are unreasonable, wrong attitudes, yet instinct will dictate them.

As I followed the crowd I also started to act like this. Instead of being a lone wolf, I became a confused, excited lamb milling around with others, waiting to be clipped. It was impossible for me to say "no" when everybody around me was saying "yes". I got scared when they got scared. I became hopeful when they were hopeful.

Nothing like this, not even in my first novice years, had ever happened to me. I lost all my skill and control. Everything I touched went wrong.

I behaved like a complete amateur. The careful system I had built up collapsed around me. Every transaction ended in disaster. I put in dozens of contradictory orders. I bought stocks at 55. They went back to 51. I hung on. Stop-loss? That was the first thing I threw away. Patience? Judgment? I had none. Boxes? I forgot about them.

As the days went by the vicious circle of my operations started to look like this:

I BOUGHT AT THE TOP As

Soon as I bought

The stock started to drop I

Became frightened

AND SOLD AT THE BOTTOM

As soon as I sold

The stock started to rise I became greedy A N D

B O U G H T A T T H E T O P

I developed a tremendous frustration. Instead of blaming my own stupidity, I invented different reasons for my failures. I started to believe in "They." "They" were selling me dear. "They" were buying stock from me cheap. I could not, of course, tell anyone who "They" were—but that did not stop me from believing in them.

Fighting "Them"—these grey ghosts at the back of the mind —made me reckless. I became stubborn. Even though stocks went on beating me, each time they hit me I just wiped off the blood and came back for more. I kept telling myself that I was more than half-a-million dollars ahead of the market and therefore this could not possibly be happening to me. How wrong I was!

It was a period of complete disaster. I lost $100,000 in a few weeks. A detailed list of my trading at this time reads like a lunatic's chronicle. I can still hardly believe it. Now I know that it was caused by egotism leading to vanity leading to over-confidence, which in turn led to disaster. It was not the market that beat me. It was my own unreasoning instincts and uncontrolled emotions.

I bought stocks and sold them a few hours later. I knew that if I bought and sold the same day, I was permitted to operate with as little as 2 5 % margin in my account. Instead of profiting from this, I succeeded in losing several thousand dollars each time. This is how I assured myself of disaster:

2,500 HAVEG INDUSTRIES

Bought at	70	($176,150.00)	
Sold at	63½	($157,891.34)	
		Loss	$ 18,258.66

1,000 ROME CABLE

Bought at	37	($ 37,375.00)	
Sold at	31	($ 30,724.48)	
		Loss	$ 6,650.52

1,000 GENERAL TIME

Bought at	47¾	($48,178.80)	
Sold at	44¾	($ 44,434.32)	
		Loss	$ 3,744.48

500 ADDRESSOGRAPH-MULTIGRAPH

Bought at	124½	($ 62,507.25)	
Sold at	116½	($ 58,053.90)	
		Loss	$ 4,453.35

1,000 REICHHOLD CHEMICALS

Bought at	63½	($ 63,953.50)	
Sold at	16½	($ 61,158.37)	
		Loss	$ 2,795.13

2,000 BRUNSWICK-BALKE-COLLENDER

Bought at	55½	($111,891.00)	
Sold at	53½	($106,443.46)	
		Loss	$ 5,447.54

2,000 RAYTHEON

Bought at	60½	($121,901.00)	
Sold at	57¾	($114,823.69)	

			Loss	$ 7,077.31
2,000 NATIONAL RESEARCH				
Bought at	24½	($ 49,625.00)		
Sold at	22	($ 43,501.52)		
			Loss	$ 6,123.48
4,000 AMERICAN METALS-CLIMAX				
Bought at	32⅞	($132,917.60)		
Sold at	31⅝	($125,430.47)		
			Loss	$ 7,487.13
3,000 AMERICAN MOTORS				
Bought at	41¼	($124,938.90)		
Sold at	40	($119,094.60)		
			Loss	$ 5,844.30
2,000 MOLYBDENUM				
Bought at	49½	($ 99,875.00)		
Sold at	47½	($ 94,352.50)		
			Loss	$ 5,522.50
2,000 SHARON STEEL				
Bought at	48¼	($ 97,362.60)		
Sold at	43¼	($ 85,877.27)		
			Loss	$ 11,485.33
1,000 WARNER LAMBERT				
Bought at	98½	($ 98,988.50)		
Sold at	95½	($ 95,127.09)		
			Loss	$ 3,861.41
1,000 LUKENS STEEL				
Bought at	88	($ 88,478.00)		
Sold at	81	($ 80,640.48)		
			Loss	$ 7,837.52
		Total Loss	$ 96,588.66	

Do you wonder, after this melancholy table, why I shuddered

whenever I looked at stocks?

The plain fact was that I was reading too much, trying to do too much. That is why I rapidly reached the stage where I could read the figures on the stock market quotations but they no longer told me anything. Not long afterwards came an even worse phase. Haunted by never-ending losses, terrified by the confusion, racked by rumors, I got so I could not even see the figures. My coordination broke down. I used to pore all day over columns of figures, which my eyes scanned, but I could not assimilate. My mind had become blurred. This last phase really frightened me. I felt like a drunk who loses touch with reality and cannot understand why.

At the end of a few disastrous weeks, I sat down soberly to examine the reasons why this should have happened to me. Why should I have the touch in Hong Kong, Calcutta, Saigon and Stockholm, and lose it when I was within half a mile of Wall Street? What was the difference?

There was no easy solution to the problem and for a long time I was baffled. Then one day, as I sat in the Plaza Hotel afraid to make a telephone call, I suddenly realized something. When I was abroad, I visited no boardrooms, talked to no one, received no telephone calls, watched no ticker.

The solution was whispering to me but at first I could not credit it. It was so surprising, so simple and yet so extraordinary that I could hardly believe it. It was: My ears were my enemy.

It dawned on me like a revelation that when I was traveling abroad I had been able to assess the market, or rather the few stocks in which I was interested, calmly, neutrally, without interruption or rumor, completely without emotion and ego.

I had operated simply on the basis of my daily telegram, which gave me my perspective. It showed me the way my stocks were behaving. There were no other influences, because I did not see or hear anything else.

In New York it was nothing like that. There were interruptions, rumors, panics, contradictory information, all floating into my ear. As a result of this my emotions became involved with the stocks—and the cold, clinical approach had gone.

I decided there was only one answer. I must try to find myself. I must go away at once, a long way from New York, before I lost all my money.

There was only one thing, which saved me from complete ruin during this period. And that was that UNIVERSAL CONTROLS and THIOKOL were behaving well and I left them alone. I now realize I only did this because I was too busy to bother about them? I was trading in other stocks, which were losing me money.

I reviewed the situation and got rid of every stock except for these two. Then I took a plane for Paris. Before I left, however, I made a very important decision. I gave instructions to my brokers that they must never telephone me or give me any information of any sort on any pretext whatsoever. The only communication I wanted from them and from Wall Street was my usual daily telegram.

I wandered around Paris in a daze, my head still spinning with blurred, meaningless columns of stock market quotations. My daily telegrams arrived—and they did not make much sense to me. I had completely lost my touch. I felt like a man who has had a terrible accident and feels he will never be well again. I was thoroughly demoralized.

Then just when I thought my condition was permanent something happened. I had been in Paris about two weeks when one day I picked up my daily telegram in the Hotel Georges V. As I scanned it dispiritedly somehow the figures seemed less dim. At first I could not believe it. I felt myself gazing at them as though I had never seen them before. I was afraid I was only imagining things.

I impatiently waited for the next day's cable. When I received it, there was no doubt: the figures were clearer and more familiar. As though a veil was being lifted, once again images started to form before my eyes, giving me some view of the stock's future.

In the days that followed my telegrams became clearer and clearer; I started reading the quotes like my old self. Once more I could see that some of the stocks were stronger, others weaker. Simultaneously my "feeling" started to return. Gradually, like an invalid, I began to regain my confidence. I recovered enough courage to try to approach the market again.

But I had learned my lesson. I decided to make it a permanent rule that I must never visit a brokerage office again. Also my brokers must be prohibited from picking up the telephone and calling me. I must only have stock quotations by cable—and nothing else.

Even if I returned to the New York hotel, the scene of my disastrous dealings, which is within a short taxi ride of Wall Street, my instructions would be unyielding. I must place Wall Street thousands of miles away from me. Every day my brokers must send me a telegram just as if I were in Hong Kong, Karachi or Stockholm.

Also, my brokers must never quote any stock to me, except the ones I asked for. They must not tell me about any new stock because that would immediately come into the rumor class. I would pick new stocks myself, as I had always done, by reading my weekly financial paper. When I saw one that interested me and seemed to be preparing for a rise, I would ask for quotations. I would only ask for one new quotation at a time. Then, as I did before, I would study it carefully before deciding if it was worth going into.

Like a man who has survived a plane crash and knows he must fly again immediately or lose his nerve, I knew only one way of making this method foolproof. I booked myself on a plane back to New York.

Chapter 10

Two Million Dollars

When I came back to New York in the third week of February 1959, I had completely recovered from the shock of my mad period, and I began to invest in the market again.

I could still feel the bruises of my own foolishness but I was like a man who feels stronger and better after a bad experience. I had learned my last lesson. I knew now that I had to keep rigidly to the system I had carved out for myself. I had learned that if I deviated from it even once, I would be in trouble. My whole financial structure was immediately in danger—it could crash like a house of cards.

My first move in New York was to erect an iron fence around myself to ensure that I did not repeat any of my previous errors.

I first decided to spread out my deals among six brokers. This way my operations would not be followed. To guard myself against any possible interference from them, I put up my barrier. It is a way of protection I am still using today.

This is how I worked it out. I asked my brokers to send out their telegrams after Wall Street closing time, so they would reach me at 6

P.M. This is about the time I get up—the result of performing in nightclubs for many years. Meanwhile, during the day, the telephone operator is instructed not to let any calls through.

In this way everything happens in Wall Street while I am in bed. I am sleeping while they are working, and they cannot reach me nor worry me. My delegate, the stop-loss order, represents me in case something unforeseen happens.

At 7 P.M. I start to work studying my daily telegram and deciding what my future dealings will be. Before I do this, I buy a copy of an afternoon paper that contains Wall Street closing prices. I tear out the pages giving the day's quotations and throw the rest of the financial section away. I do not wish to read any financial stories or commentaries, however well informed. They might lead me astray.

Then, with my telegram and my page out of the newspaper, I settle down to work while Wall Street sleeps.

During the weeks I spent repairing my injured confidence, the two stocks I did not sell continued to rise, UNIVERSAL CONTROLS almost uninterruptedly advanced until it stood around 60. This was more than a 40% rise since my last New York visit. THIOKOL behaved equally well and now was pushing over 110.

This was very promising indeed. I decided I had no reason whatever to touch them. Armed by my bitter experience and well entrenched behind my new strong fence, I began to move into the market with cautious confidence.

These were some of my successful operations:

I,000 GENERAL TIRE & RUBBER

Bought at	56	($56,446.00)	
Sold at	69½	($69,151.01)	
			Profit $12,705.01

1,000 CENCO INSTRUMENTS

Bought at	19½	($19,775.00)	
Sold at	23½	($23,247.63)	
			Profit $ 3,472.63

500 AMERICAN PHOTOCOPY

Bought at	71½	($35,980.75)
Sold at	79½	($39,570.92)
		Profit $ 3,590.17

1,000 UNION OIL OF CALIF

Bought at	46	($46,420.00)
Sold at	50	($49,669.00)
		Profit $ 3,249.00

500 POLAROID

Bought at	121	($60,755.50)
Sold at	127	($63,299.08)
		Profit $ 2,543.58

500 BRUNSWICK-BALKE-COLLENDER

Bought at	71¼	($35, 855.6 5)
Sold at	77	($38,322.08)
		Profit $ 2,466.43

500 BELL & HO WELL

Bought at	93	($46,741.50)
Sold at	99¼	($49,436.81)
		Profit $ 2,695.3

This being the stock market, not all my deals were successful. A number of stocks I bought did not behave as I had predicted.

These are some of my transactions ending with a loss:

1,000 CENCO INSTRUMENTS

Bought at	23	($23,300.00)
Sold at	22	($21,755.76)
		Loss $ 1,544.24

500 REICHHOLD CHEMICALS

Bought at	65	($32,727.50)
Sold at	63%	($31,703.17)
		Loss $ 1,024.33

1,000 FANSTEEL

Bought at	63½	($63,953.50)	
Sold at	62	($61,6S7.96)	
			Loss $ 2,295.54

500 PHILADELPHIA & READING

Bought at	131	($65,760.50)	
Sold at	129¾	($64,672.79)	
			Loss $ 1,087.71

These two tables confirm my method completely. You will notice that in each case I was successful in taking larger profits than losses in proportion to the amounts invested. Remember that all these operations were entirely done by telegram from New York to New York. I had never seen or spoken to my brokers even once. Many times during the day's trading when some of my holdings began to flutter and fail like dying birds, they must have itched to pick up a telephone and alert me. They must have felt I was the biggest fool in the world to forbid them to do it. But my rule was rigid. I heard the news—good or bad —every day at 6 P.M. when my telegrams arrived. Then I began to act.

During the few weeks I spent trading like this in New York, signs of trouble started to show up in UNIVERSAL CONTROLS. It began to lose its steady upward marching progress. Its activity and price advance became wild—too wild.

This spelled trouble and trouble surely came. After an advance from 66 in the first week of March, the stock rose within three weeks to 102. It was at this point that it switched its momentum and began to go in the other direction. I did not like the look of this drop at all. It fell as if in an air pocket and there seemed no sign of a rise. I had little doubt that the holiday was over. If I were not careful I might get caught in a nose- dive, so I brought up my stop-loss within two points of the day's closing price. I was sold out of UNIVERSAL CONTROLS next morning at varying prices between 86% and 89%. This was more than 12 points from the high. I was well content with this. There was no reason why I should be unhappy. I had had a good long ride and my total selling price was $524,669.97. This gave me a profit of $409,356.48.

I now had a very large capital to invest. I took a careful look at the market, looking as usual for an actively traded, high-priced stock. Another problem arose at this point which made a suitable stock more difficult to find. With this amount of money to spend I must be careful not to allow my own buying unduly to influence the market

After some search I alighted on a stock, which fulfilled all these difficult requirements. It was TEXAS INSTRUMENTS.

I bought my first 2,000 shares at an average price of 94⅜ in the second week of April and another 1,500 at 97⅞. As the stock continued to act well, I added to my holdings 2,000 shares.

The average price of this last purchase was 101 %. This, as you realize, involved big money, more than half a million dollars in fact. The details of my TEXAS INSTRUMENTS purchases looked like this:

2,000 shares at	94¾	$189,718.80
1,500 shares at	97⅞	$147,544.35
2,000 shares at	101⅞	$204,733.80
Total 5,500 shares		$541,996.95

Now that the capital I had taken out of UNIVERSAL CONTROLS was reinvested, I devoted my attention once again to THIOKOL.

THIOKOL and I were now partners of long standing and had, like all old- time partners, a special relationship. I had always allowed THIOKOL a greater leeway than other stocks—partly because I really "felt" this stock, and also because I had the great advantage afforded by the special subscription account.

It would have been foolish to give up such a unique credit arrangement, so I always kept my trailing stop-loss far behind its rise. This I would do with no other stock, but in the case of THIOKOL it saved me twice from being sold out. The second time was when it had a very bad reaction in the first week of April. This reaction came on the heels of the announcement of a 3-for-l split. It was so severe that I thought we would have to part, but I decided to let my stop-loss decide.

This was not touched off, and the sinking spell was quickly followed by a vigorous rise. However, I was not the only one who liked THIOKOL. The newly split stock was met by a hectic public response which shot it up to 72 in the first week of May.

The response was too good. It led to this amazing situation:

Its activity for the week was an incredible volume of 549,400 shares.

Its advance for the week was 13¼ points.

The trading volume represented an aggregate value of $40,000,000.

The price difference for the week was $7,000,000.

It looked as if every trader on the New York Stock Exchange had done nothing else all week but rush in and out of THIOKOL.

Of course, it could not last. The governors of the New York Stock Exchange decided to suspend all stop orders. The effect of this was that the majority of traders left the stock alone. They would not buy and sell a stock where they could not protect themselves. It also meant that I was automatically out of the stock myself. They had taken my most powerful tool away, and I could not work without it.

I sold my THIOKOL holdings, at an average price of 68. This gave me, under the 3-for-l split, over $200 for each of my original 6,000 shares. I had paid a total of $350,820. For my 18,000 split shares I received $1,212,851.52. My profit was $862,031.52.

The prospect of putting a million dollars back into the market posed an enormous problem. I would have to be doubly careful.

This was too much money to switch into another stock easily. It was such a big sum that my buy was bound to influence the market.

I also had to face the fact that my stop-loss would be no longer practical, because no trader or specialist would absorb such a large quantity of stock in a matter of seconds.

There was only one thing to do: I decided to divide my funds into two parts. Once I had made up my mind to do this, selection was comparatively easy. I had only to decide among four stocks:

ZENITH RADIO, LITTON INDUSTRIES, FAIRCHILD CAMERA and BECKMAN INSTRUMENTS.

I had watched all of these for a long time. They were all suitable as far as my techno-fundamentalist theories were concerned. Now all that remained was to see which two of them I should choose. There was only one way to do this—to let their strength in the market be the judge.

Using the technique I had employed so successfully with UNIVERSAL CONTROLS and THIOKOL, I made a pilot buy into all four of them on May 13, 1959:

500 shares ZENITH RADIO	at	104	($52,247)
500 shares BECKMAN INSTRUMENTS	at	66	($3 3,228)
500 shares FAIRCHILD CAMERA	at	128	($64,259)
500 shares LITTON INDUSTRIES	at	112	($ 56,251)

On each of these stocks I put a stop-loss order of 10 per cent below buying price.

I was fully aware that these stop-losses were vague and too mechanical. It was a deliberate, if clumsy, method. I purposely used this system because I knew sooner or later it would eliminate those of the four that were weakest.

On May 18th I was stopped out of BECKMAN INSTRUMENTS at 60, and on May 19th I decided to sell LITTON INDUSTRIES, which was acting worse than the others, at 106¼. Now I adjusted my stop-losses on the remaining stocks.

It was the fourth week of May when I proceeded to switch more than $1,000,000 into the two stronger stocks. These were my total purchases:

ZENITH RADIO

500 shares a	104	$ 52,247.00
1,500 shares at	99¾	150,359.70
1,000 shares at	104	104,494.00
1,000 shares at	105¼	105,745.30
1,500 shares at	107½	161,996.25
Total 5,500 shares		$574,842.25

FAIRCHILD CAMERA

500 shares at	128	$64,259.00
1,000 shares at	123¼	123,763.30
1,000 shares at	125	125,515.00
1,000 shares at	126¼	126,766.30
1,000 shares at	127	127,517.00
Total 4,500 shares		$567,820.60

Discounting my short-term tradings, my funds were switched from stock to stock in the following way:

March-April 1959

Sold	UNIVERSAL CONTROLS	$524,670	
Bought	TEXAS INSTRUMENTS		$ 541,997

May 1959

Sold	THIOKOL CHEMICAL	$1,212,850	
Bought	ZENITHRADIO		$ 574,842
Bought	FAIRCHILD CAMERA		$ 567,821
	Total received		$1,737,520
	Margin debt		274,600
			$1,462,920
	Available cash from previous operations		70,000
	Available for reinvestment		$1,532,920
	Total reinvested (at 90% margin)		$1,684,660

At that time I had six brokers. I closed my account with three of them. Then I sat back and watched the stocks I held. There was nothing else for me to do while TEXAS INSTRUMENTS, ZENITH RADIO and FAIRCHILD CAMERA went to work for me.

During June the telegrams continued to flash between Wall Street and the Plaza Hotel. They were meaningless to the Western Union operators but they were full of meaning for me. For instance, on June 9th I received the following telegram:

"Z 122½ (124-116¾) T 119¼ (121½-117¼) F 125 (126-121)"

The following day's telegram read:

"Z 132⅜ (132½-125) T 123¾ (123⅞-120⅜) F 130 (130-126½)"

They were boring, meaningless hieroglyphics to the operator but they meant a lot to me. They told me that the value of my holdings had appreciated $100,000 in that one single day!

It began to be a strange life. I sat in the Plaza every evening, reading my telegram and filing it. There was nothing further I could do. I felt elated and restless, but powerless. I was like a scientist who, after years of work and research, has successfully launched a rocket to the moon, and now as he tracks it climbing higher and higher he has a tremendous sense of achievement and also a strange letdown feeling of inactivity.

Like him, I was now on the sidelines just keeping vigil while my stocks continued to climb steadily like well-made missiles.

Then one day early in July I received an offer to appear in the "Sporting Club" in Monte Carlo. I accepted it gladly. Sitting still was beginning to hold a slight boredom after all my nerve-wracking problems and panics of the past.

Before making arrangements to leave New York I asked my brokers to meet me. I went through my accounts with each of them. I found that if I were to sell out before flying to Europe I could realize my stocks for over $2,250,000.

What was my feeling at this news? Elation? Excitement that I was now more than twice a millionaire? Not exactly. I was happy, but not excited. I had been much more excited when I made my first $10,000 out of DINERS' CLUB. This time I felt rather like a runner who has trained strenuously and has suffered many defeats, and now trots to victory.

I was also faced with the same dilemma I had known before: Should I sell? Should I get out altogether?

The answer this time was easy. It was the old tried and trusted answer: I did not have any reason to sell a rising stock. I would just continue to jog along with the trend, trailing my stop-loss behind me. As the trend increased, I would buy more. If the trend reversed? I would, as ever, flee like a disturbed burglar.

I put new stop-losses on all my stocks so that if they dropped while I was on my way to Europe I would be sold out and my two million would remain intact.

I felt content and assured as I rode up Fifth Avenue in a taxi after leaving my brokers.

I walked into the lobby of the Plaza Hotel, automatically bought an evening paper, tore out the Wall Street closing prices, threw the rest of the newspaper away, picked up my 6 P.M. telegram and went up in the elevator.

In my room I opened the telegram, spread out the sheet of newspaper, and sat back with a happy sigh. Not only because I had made two million dollars but because I was doing what I liked best.

I was working while Wall Street slept.

■ □ ■ □ $ □ ■ □ ■

Interview With Time Magazine

It was May 1959—six-and-a-half years after I had been offered the Canadian stock called BRILUND by the Smith brothers. It looked as though the wheel had turned full circle because, like then, I was again appearing at the "Latin Quarter" in New York.

Somehow my stock-market dealings had got talked about in Wall Street. The news of my success had leaked out and gradually spread.

One day, to my surprise, I received a telephone call from the Business Section of Time. They said they had heard something about my success in the market and asked if they could send a reporter to see me.

Next day he came and I gave him all the facts about how I had made my fortune. I let him see my accounts, my statements, my cables. He examined them carefully and left saying that he was very impressed with my story.

A day later he came back and told me the business experts on the staff were highly skeptical. They said the story could not be true.

This really did not surprise me, so again I took him over the facts and figures. He studied them for several hours, and when he finally went away he seemed to be convinced that they were accurate.

But this, I was to discover, was only the preliminary skirmish. The next morning he called to ask if we could meet for lunch. Half an hour before lunch, he telephoned again and said he was bringing along a senior editor, who wanted to check on the story himself.

They arrived for lunch at one o'clock. Once again I went through all the financial details. The senior editor was so interested that he left his food untouched on the table.

At four o'clock, after he had heard the whole story, he ate a sandwich. At five o'clock he left with the reporter. He had made no comment, but he was obviously impressed. I have never seen a man so interested.

At six o'clock that evening came another phone call. This time it was a Wall Street expert of Time. He said the Managing Editor would not allow the story to be printed until three members of the Time staff would vouch collectively that they had seen me and checked all the facts. He also, to my great surprise, insisted on seeing my dancing act.

The Managing Editor not only doubted my success in the stock market, but he apparently did not think I could dance either!

At seven o'clock the expert arrived. At first he shook his head incredulously about everything I told him and all the evidence. I produced concerning my stock-market operations. He seemed determined to disbelieve everything.

When Julia and I appeared on stage he seemed to be impressed by our dancing—so at least that was something! I had been undergoing this cross-examination for three days and I was becoming slightly unnerved by it. As a result I did not feel at the top of my form and towards the end of the act, when I had a strenuous lift to perform, I tore one of my right arm muscles badly. I was just able to finish the act.

It was with a painfully aching arm that I sat down with the Wall Street expert to continue the meticulous financial cross-examination.

It went on and on—for hours. All the time he came back to one question: Why did I talk so freely about my stock transactions?

I replied that it was because I was proud of what I had been able to do. I felt that I had nothing to hide.

It was after midnight, but during all these hours my inquisitor refused to have even one drink. He admitted, quite frankly, that he wanted to keep his mind clear to detect any flaws in my system or records.

Then at two in the morning, he threw down his ballpoint. "Let's have a drink," he said. His last skeptical doubt had been swept away. He was convinced. He lifted his glass and toasted my success in the market.

He left at four o'clock in the morning, but before he did he was asking me for advice. I gave it to him. I told him to buy a certain stock, but only if it rose to 3954. He was also to put a stop-loss on it of 38^4. I hope he did not disregard this advice and buy at a lower figure because it never reached 39%. It fell suddenly to 22!

The following week the article appeared in Time, which of course has a highly influential readership, especially in financial circles. The result was that I became accepted by most—but not all—of the financial pundits as a highly successful, if unorthodox, stock-market investor. Hence this book.

The other result was that I had a badly torn muscle. A doctor told me that I might have to stop performing the act altogether. He was doubtful if I would ever be able to lift my partner again.

Two weeks later I was on the stage doing the act as usual. I have done it ever since—proving, perhaps, that medical experts can sometimes be as wrong as the experts on Wall Street.

■ □ ■ □ $ □ ■ □ ■

APPENDIX

Cables

His two-year dancing tour of the world forced Darvas to rely exclusively on cablegrams as a means of communication between himself and Wall Street. Despite the many inconveniences that were involved, this turned out to be an important element in the combination of investment techniques that led to his eventual success in the stock market.

The following are reproductions of actual cables that show just how he was able to transact his stock-market operations from any part of the world. They include typical examples of the various phases of these transactions.

Once Darvas had instructed his broker as to which stocks he wanted quoted, only the initial letters of the names were necessary. It was the code-like nature of these messages that led to frequent difficulties with cable-office employees.

The upper cable is one he received in Karachi, Pakistan, notifying him that his broker had executed an on-stop purchase order. At the same time, the day's closing, high and low prices were listed for the other stocks in which Darvas was interested at the time—THIOKOL CHEMICAL, POLAROID, UNIVERSAL CONTROLS and LITTON INDUSTRIES.

When Darvas placed a buy order, he usually gave the full name of the stock. In the lower cable, from Phnompenh in Indochina, he transmitted a "good-till-cancelled" on-stop order for 500 shares of CENCO INSTRUMENTS at 7¼ and 200 LORIL-LARD at 31¼. In both cases he automatically included stop-losses (6 1/8 and 29⅝ respectively), as was his practice. In addition, he brought his broker up to date on his next change of address, and requested the day's closing prices of CENCO, HERTZ, THIOKOL and LORILLARP.

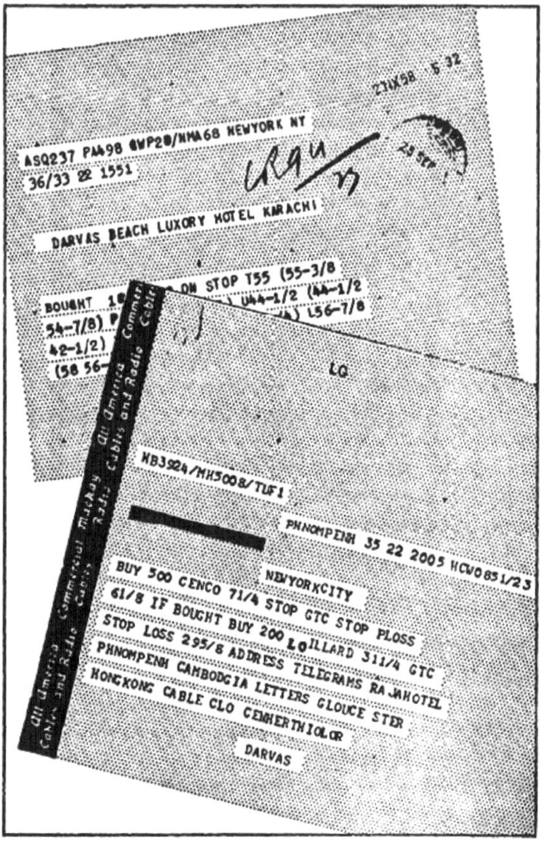
ASQ237 PA498 GWP28/NMA68 NEWYORK NY
36/33 22 1551
DARVAS BEACH LUXORY HOTEL KARACHI
BOUGHT 1... ON STOP T55 (55-3/8
54-7/8) P... U44-1/2 (44-1/2
42-1/2) ... L56-7/8
(58 56-...

HB3924/MH5008/TUF1
PHNOMPENH 35 22 2005 HCV0851/23
NEWYORKCITY
BUY 500 CENCO 71/4 STOP GTC STOP PLOSS
61/8 IF BOUGHT BUY 200 LORILLARD 311/4 GTC
STOP LOSS 295/8 ADDRESS TELEGRAMS RAJAHOTEL
PHNOMPENH CAMBODGIA LETTERS GLOUCESTER
HONGKONG CABLE CLO CENHERTHIOLOR
DARVAS

With his automatic stop-loss accompanying every buy order, Darvas was frequently in and out of a stock in one day. In the top cable, received in Paris, he was informed that 500 shares of a stock had been bought and later sold as the price dropped to his stop-loss point of 53⅞. Another purchase was confirmed, and the day's quotations supplied for BOEING, LITTON INDUSTRIES and several other stocks. The final figure represents the Dow-Jones Industrial Average for that day in abbreviated form.

Darvas was constantly changing or cancelling orders on the basis of his daily quotes. In the center cable, from Nagoya, Japan, he instructed his broker to raise the quantity of a previous DINERS' CLUB order. He later cancelled this particular order altogether.

Aside from the daily wires, Darvas' only contact with Wall Street was Barron's, which was airmailed to him every week as soon as it was published. The bottom cable, from Saigon in Indochina, reflects his complete dependence on regular receipt of this publication.

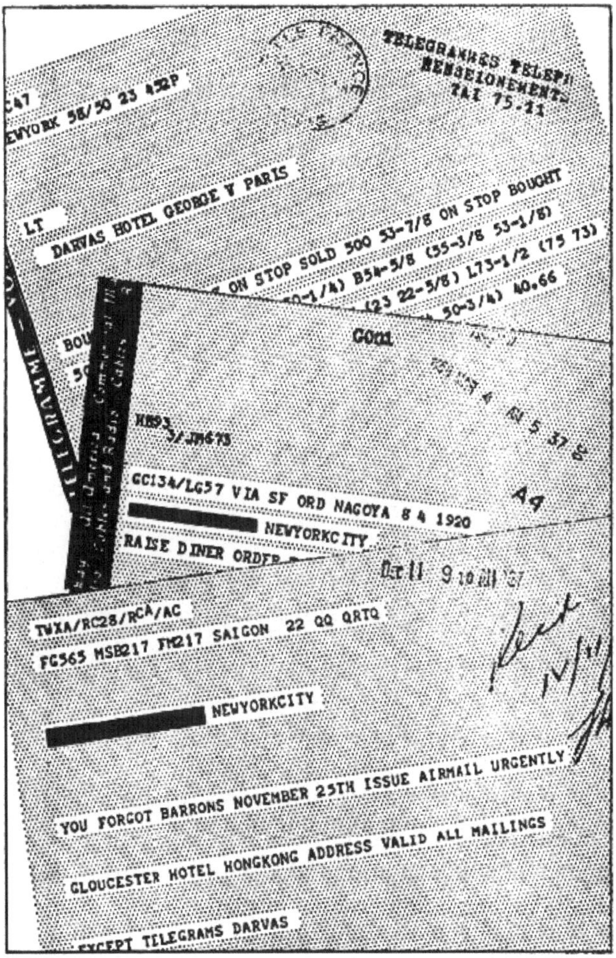

LT
DARVAS HOTEL GEORGE V PARIS

CC134/LG57 VIA SF ORD NAGOYA 8 4 1920
NEWYORKCITY
RAISE DINER ORDER

TWXA/RC28/RCA/AC
FC565 MSB217 FM217 SAIGON 22 QQ QRTQ
NEWYORKCITY
YOU FORGOT BARRONS NOVEMBER 25TH ISSUE AIRMAIL URGENTLY
GLOUCESTER HOTEL HONGKONG ADDRESS VALID ALL MAILINGS
EXCEPT TELEGRAMS DARVAS

Darvas was always fearful that a vitally important cable calling for immediate action might miss him in transit. This problem was solved when he realized he could instruct his broken to send copies of a cable to both the airport at which he would be changing planes and the hotel at which he was to arrive.

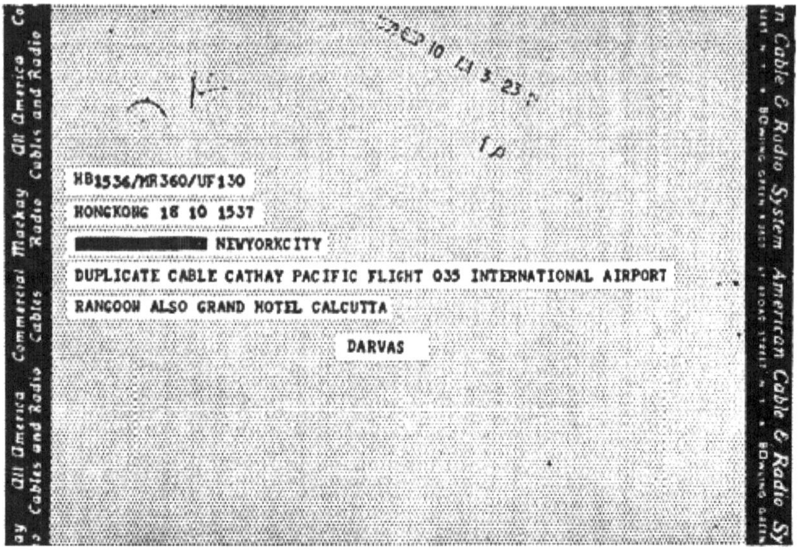
HB1536/MR360/UF130
HONGKONG 18 10 1537
NEWYORKCITY
DUPLICATE CABLE CATHAY PACIFIC FLIGHT 035 INTERNATIONAL AIRPORT
RANGOON ALSO GRAND HOTEL CALCUTTA
DARVAS

An on-stop buy order cannot always be executed at one price for the entire number of shares. According to the market, the purchase is made in hundred lots at varying prices starting at or above the specified buy price.

According to this cable received at Kathmandu, Nepal, Darvas1 order for 500 PARMELEE TRANSPORTATION had been filled at two prices: 400 shares at 3 3 ½ and 100 at 33¾. The stock had closed at 34 1/8 and its range for the day was 34½-32⅝.

Darvas says that this cable is unusually intelligible compared to many of the handwritten messages he had to call for at the Indian Embassy, which had the only telegraphic link with the outside world. The day's quotes are clear enough for PARMELEE, THIOKOL, UNIVERSAL CONTROLS, FAIRCHILD CAMERA and LITTON INDUSTRIES. As for the last stock, Darvas cannot identify it now, although he must have known at the time what it was supposed to be.

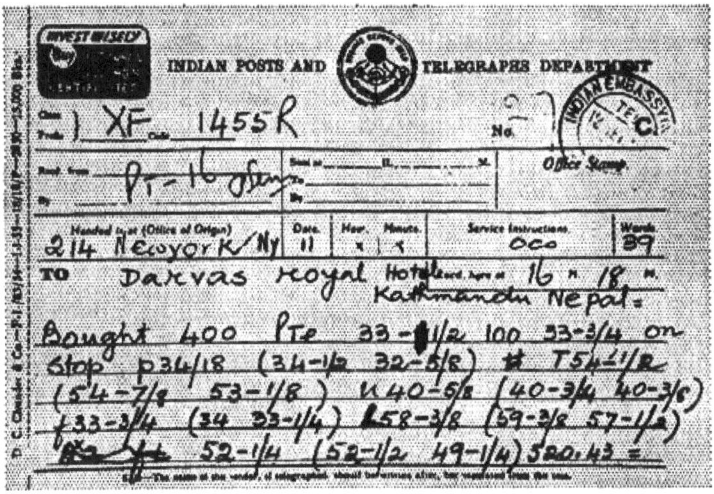

INDIAN POSTS AND TELEGRAPHS DEPARTMENT

1 XF 1455R

214 NewyorK/NY 11 39

TO Darvas Royal Hotel 16 18 Kathmandu Nepal

Bought 400 PTE 33-1/2 100 33-3/4 on Stop P34/18 (34-1/2 32-5/8) # T54-1/2 (54-7/8 53-1/8) U40-5/8 (40-3/4 40-3/8) 33-3/4 (34 33-1/4) 58-3/8 (59-3/8 57-1/2) 52-1/4 (52-1/2 49-1/4) 520.43

Darvas first became interested in a particular stock on the basis of its movement as recorded in Barton's. Since this publication took several days to reach him, he needed to be brought up to date by cable concerning the most recent activity of the stock.

It was in Hong Kong that he first noticed the unusual amount of trading in the stock of a small company, and from there he sent this cable requesting "this week's range and closing price of E. L. BRUCE". Little did he suspect then that his pinpointing of this stock on purely technical grounds was to result in a profit of almost $300,000?

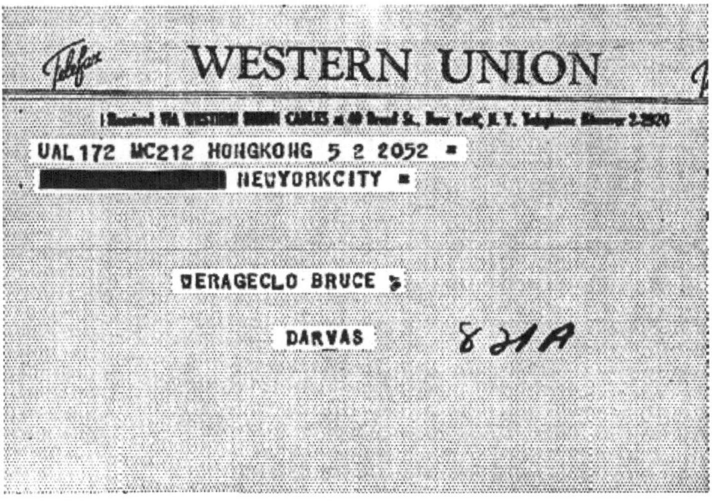

WESTERN UNION

UAL172 MC212 HONGKONG 5 2 2052

NEWYORKCITY

WERAGECLO BRUCE

DARVAS 821A

Once the daily quotes on a stock showed Darvas that it was following the pattern his theory called for, he would generally make a small pilot buy. It was only when he actually owned shares that he could really get the "feel" of the stock's movements. Since his broker had blanket instructions to handle all of Darvas' on-stop orders on a good-till- cancelled basis, he often specifically placed a "day order" for a pilot buy.

These few words from New Delhi, ordering 200 shares of THIOKOL CHEMICAL at 47¼, were to be worth almost a million dollars. This pilot buy led to the eventual sale of Darvas' holdings in this one stock alone for over $1,000,000.

In this cable, Darvas also took the opportunity to raise the quantity of a UNIVERSAL PRODUCTS order, only to cancel it shortly afterwards because he felt the time wasn't ripe. Within the next four weeks he actually did purchase 3,000 shares of this stock.

The last request calls for the previous week's range of EASTERN STAINLESS STEEL.

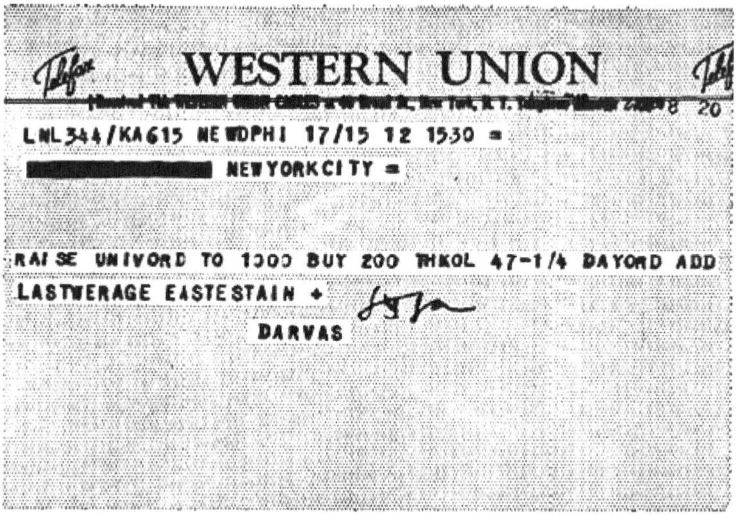
WESTERN UNION

LNL344/KA615 NEWDPHI 17/15 12 1530 =

NEWYORKCITY =

RAISE UNIVORD TO 1000 BUY 200 THKOL 47-1/4 DAYORD ADD
LASTWERAGE EASTESTAIN +
DARVAS

After his pilot buy into a stock, if the price pattern he was looking for continued consistently, Darvas followed through with additional purchases.

In this cable from Kobe, Japan, he sent the third of his orders to buy another 200 shares of LORILLARD. Darvas' purchases into this stock formed the cornerstone of the pyramid of investments that was to grow to over $2,000,000 in the following eighteen months.

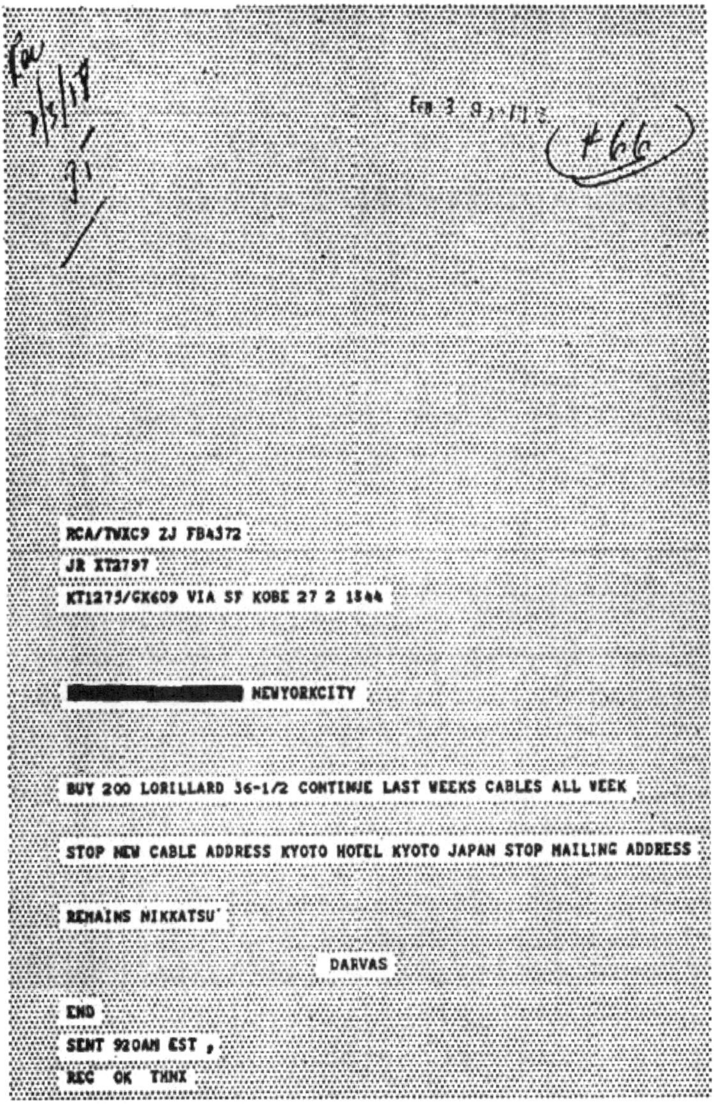

(#66)

RCA/TWXC9 ZJ FB4372
JR XT2797
KT1275/GK609 VIA SF KOBE 27 2 1544

[redacted] NEWYORKCITY

BUY 200 LORILLARD 36-1/2 CONTINUE LAST WEEKS CABLES ALL WEEK
STOP NEW CABLE ADDRESS KYOTO HOTEL KYOTO JAPAN STOP MAILING ADDRESS
REMAINS NIKKATSU

DARVAS

END
SENT 920AM EST ,
REC OK THNX

As his capital grew, so did the amount Darvas invested in any one stock once he was sure of it. After a pilot buy of 300 shares of UNIVERSAL PRODUCTS at 35¼, Darvas was well enough satisfied with the continuing movement of this little-known stock to make a second purchase of 1,200 shares.

This cable notified him that his on-stop order had been filled at the designated price of 36½, and gave him the day's range and close for UNIVERSAL.

Also quoted were HUMBLE OIL, EASTERN STAINLESS STEEL, LITTON INDUSTRIES, THIOKOL and FAIRCHILD CAMERA. For the last stock, only the "28" applies. The 3 . 5 8 stands for the Dow-Jones Average of 503.58.

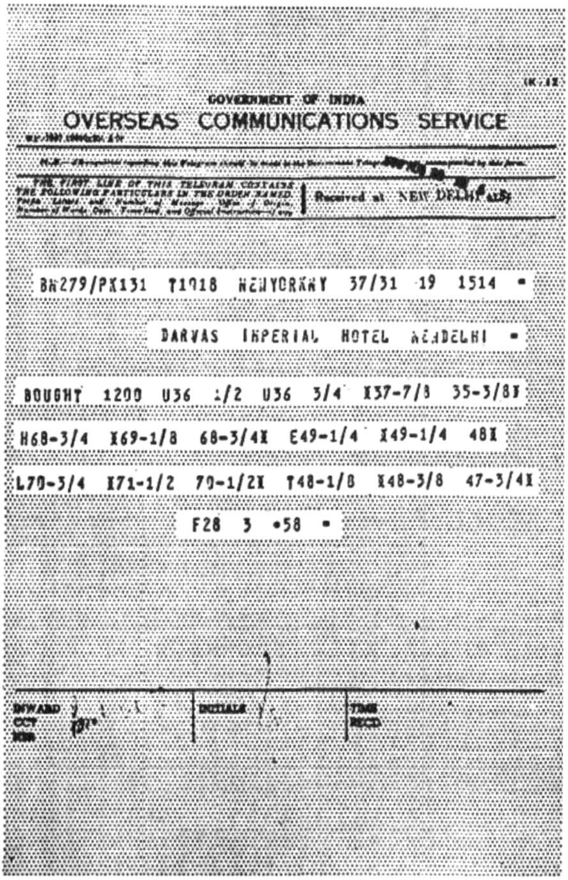
GOVERNMENT OF INDIA
OVERSEAS COMMUNICATIONS SERVICE

THE FIRST LINE OF THIS TELEGRAM CONTAINS THE FOLLOWING PARTICULARS IN THE ORDER NAMED.

Received at NEW DELHI

BH279/PX131 T1918 NEWYORKNY 37/31 19 1514 •

DARVAS IMPERIAL HOTEL NEWDELHI •

BOUGHT 1200 U36 1/2 U36 3/4 X37-7/8 35-3/8X

H68-3/4 X69-1/8 68-3/4X E49-1/4 X49-1/4 48X

L70-3/4 X71-1/2 70-1/2X T48-1/8 X48-3/8 47-3/4X

F28 3 •58 •

INWARD CCT NOS. | INITIALS | TIME RECD

After Darvas had invested in a stock, he was always careful to trail his stop-loss behind the rise. The relationship between the price and his stop-loss point was a very flexible one, since it depended on many variable factors.

He was in Hong Kong at the beginning of April 1958 when he became uncomfortable about the behavior of DINERS' CLUB, which until then had been rising steadily.

With this cable he established the very close stop-loss that was to take him out of DINERS' CLUB at a substantial profit just when this stock took a sudden and drastic turn for the worse.

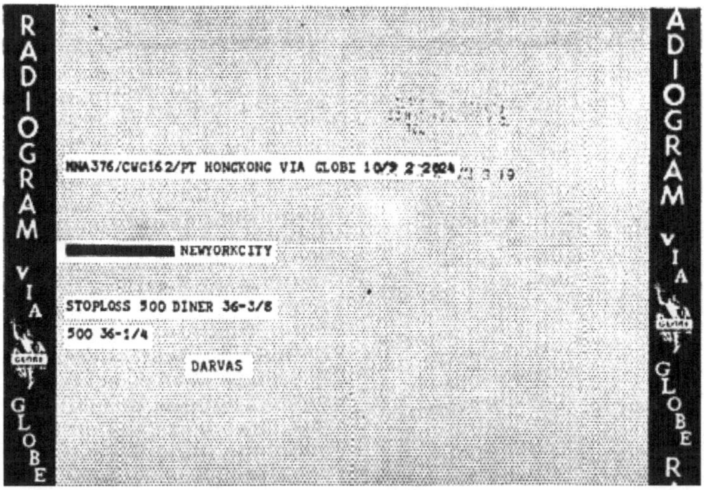
RADIOGRAM VIA GLOBE

MNA376/CWC162/PT HONGKONG VIA GLOBE 10/9 2 2024

NEWYORKCITY

STOPLOSS 500 DINER 36-3/8
500 36-1/4

DARVAS

■ □ ■ □ $ □ ■ □ ■

Charts

In the following pages the AMERICAN RESEARCH COUNCIL presents a series of specially prepared charts of weekly prices and volume for the major stocks that netted Nicolas Darvas $2,000,000. While this amount was accumulated by Darvas in a little over 18 months, we have included the record for a full three-year period—1957 through 1959—to show the history of each stock's movements before and after, as well as during, the time that Darvas held it.

In addition, explanatory notes by our editors highlight the reasoning behind Darvas' choice of each stock, the timing of his buys, and his use of the trailing stop-loss—based on his techno-fundamentalist theory as explained in the text of the book.

The charts are arranged in the order in which the stocks are discussed in the book so that the reader may more easily follow the sequence of Darvas' transactions as they occurred.

LORILLARD

Darvas asked for daily quotes on this stock after observing the sudden rise in volume at (A) when it "began to emerge from the swamp of sinking stocks like a beacon."

He bought his first 200 shares of LORILLARD at 27½ (B) with the very narrow stop-loss of 26. A few days later a sudden drop (C) touched off this stop-loss and he was sold out.

The immediate rise, which followed, convinced Darvas that his first assessment was correct, and he bought his 200 shares again at 28¾ (D).

As the "boxes" piled up, Darvas bought another 400 shares at 35 and 36½ (E). The stock rose rapidly to a new high of 44⅜.

A sudden drop to a low of 36¾ on February 18th scared him into raising his stop-loss to 36. This was not touched off, and the stock picked up momentum immediately, so he purchased a final lot of 400 shares at 38⅝ (F)*

As LORILLARD continued its sensational rise in price and volume, Darvas was strongly tempted to sell for a quick profit. But he adhered to one of the basic principles of his theory— "There is no reason to sell a rising stock"—and trailed his stop-loss at a safe distance behind the rise.

Except for the possibility that, with a very close stop-loss, he might have been sold out in June when there was a sudden drop to 53⅜, Darvas might easily have continued with LORILLARD on its phenomenal rise into the 80's at the end of the year.

However, in May he became extremely interested in the movements of another stock for which he would need all the capital he could get. It was for this reason that he sold his 1,000 shares of LORILLARD early in May at 57⅜ (G) for a substantial profit of $21,000. He was now ready to invest in E. L. BRUCE.

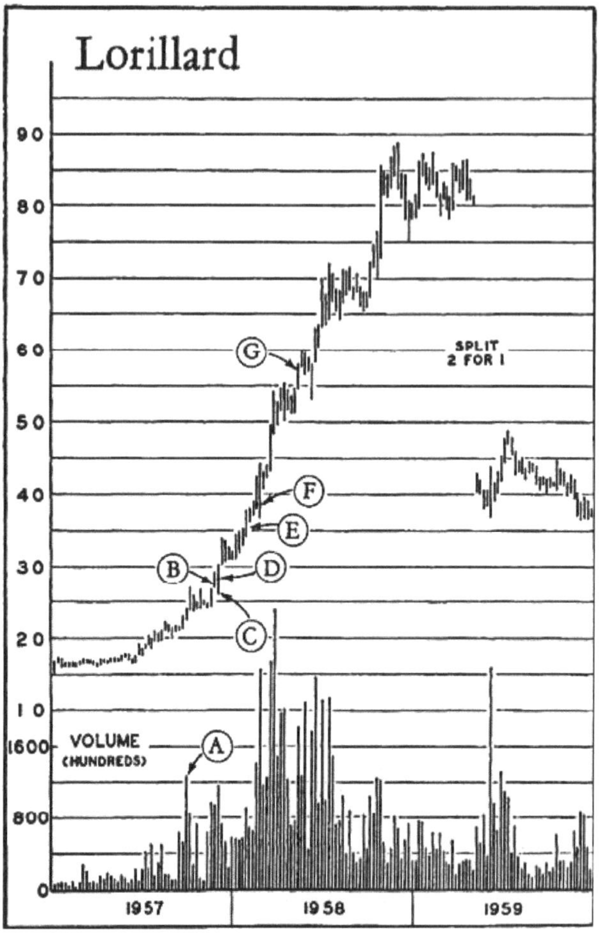

DINERS' CLUB

Although this stock had shown a rising price pattern in the first half of 1957, this rise was not marked by an accompanying increase in volume. It was only at (A), when after a 2-for-l split there was a sudden sharp jump in volume, that Darvas became seriously interested in DINERS' CLUB. He found that the company was a pioneer in a new field with a definite upward trend in earning power.

Satisfied on this "fundamental" point, he bought 500 shares at 24½ (B). As the stock continued to advance, he followed through with another 500 at 26 1/8 within a few days (C). He watched complacently as the pattern of pyramiding "boxes" developed, accompanied by a tremendous rise in trading volume. As the price rose, so did his stop- loss—to 27, then to 31.

After reaching a new high of 40½, the stock suddenly seemed to Darvas to have "lost its will to rise. It looked as if its last pyramid would hesitate on the brink of going into reverse. It almost seemed ready to tumble." Fearing collapse, Darvas moved up his stop-loss to 3654.

In the fourth week of April, "the event against which I had insured myself occurred." DINERS' CLUB took a dive and Darvas was sold out at (D), with a profit of over $10,000.

He had acted on purely technical grounds, completely unaware at the time that American Express was about to enter the credit-card field in direct competition with DINERS' CLUB. It was the successful timing of this operation that fully confirmed for him the correctness of the technical side of his approach.

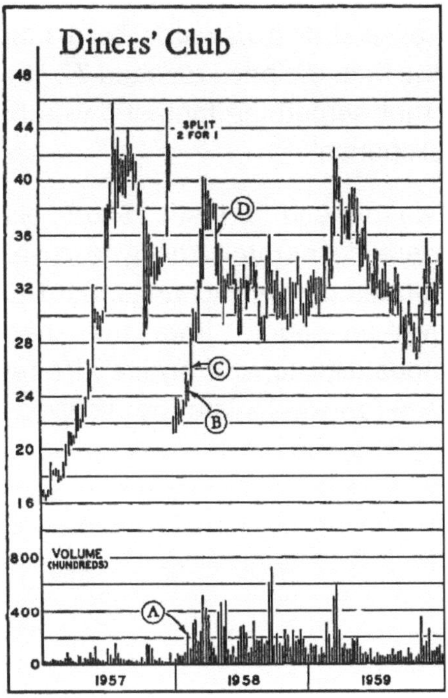

E.L.BRUCE

At the time that he had all his funds invested in LORILLARD and DINERS' CLUB, Daryas suddenly noticed (A) "a great interest springing up in a stock called E. L. BRUCE, a small Memphis firm". While it did not meet his qualifications as to fundamentals, "the technical pattern was so compelling that I could not take my eyes off it".

A phenomenal rise from 18 to 50 was followed by a reaction to 43½, but to Darvas' trained eye this seemed "only a temporary halt, a refueling". Despite the lack of a fundamental reason, he determined to buy as much as he could if it went over 50. Fully confident that the "rhythm of the advance was there", he sold out LORILLARD in order to have all his funds available for immediate investment in BRUCE.

Within a period of three weeks at the end of March, he bought a total of 2,500 shares at an average price of 52 (B).

His timing, as the chart shows, turned out to be perfect. BRUCE "began to climb as if drawn upwards by a magnet . . . It was spectacular". By the time the price reached 77 "it was obvious even in faraway India that something fantastic was happening on the American Stock Exchange".

The situation was indeed fantastic. Short-sellers operating on a "value" basis were desperately trying to cover their positions. Trading was suspended on the Exchange, but Darvas was offered $100 per share over- the-counter. It was then that he made "one of the most momentous decisions of my life". He refused to sell this "advancing stock". A few weeks later he received prices averaging 171 for a profit of $295,000.

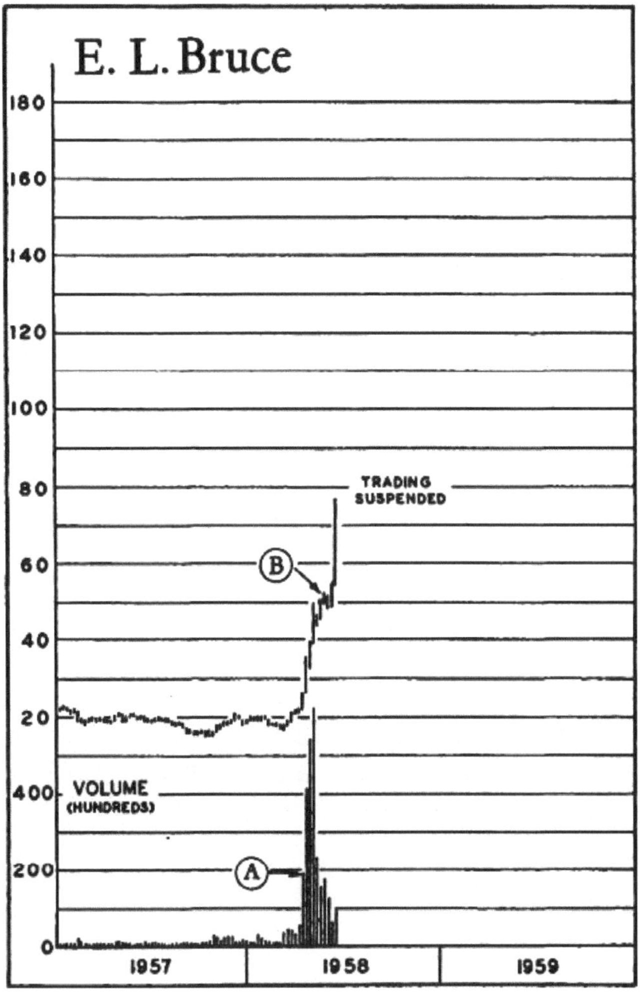

UNIRVASAL CONTROLS

"A little, unknown company called UNIVERSAL PRODUCTS" caught Darvas' eye in July 1958, after a sudden enormous spurt in volume (A) was accompanied by a price rise from below 30 into a 32-36 range.

In the beginning of August he made a cautious pilot buy of 300 shares at 35¼ (B). Two weeks later, as the stock began to "firm up", he purchased 1,200 shares at 36½ (C). Up it went, and days later he acquired 1,500 more at 40 (D).

Shortly afterwards, the company's name was changed to UNIVERSAL CONTROLS and the stock was split 2-for-l, so that he now had 6,000 shares.

In January 1959 Darvas landed in New York and embarked on a series of operations that came near to ruining him. Fortunately, UNIVERSAL CONTROLS performed beautifully during this period and gave him not a moment's concern.

But in March something began to happen to UNIVERSAL that "spelled trouble and trouble surely came". After a wild 3-week rocketing from 66 to 102, "it switched its momentum and began to go in the other direction. I did not like the look of this drop at all. It fell as if in an air-pocket and there seemed no sign of a rise."

Darvas performed exactly as he had done with DINERS' CLUB in a similar situation. He raised his stop-loss to just below the last closing price and was sold out (E). His prices, ranging from 86¼ to 89¾, were more than 12 points below the high but he was "well content with this. There was no reason why I should be unhappy. I had had a good long ride and . . . a profit of $409,000."

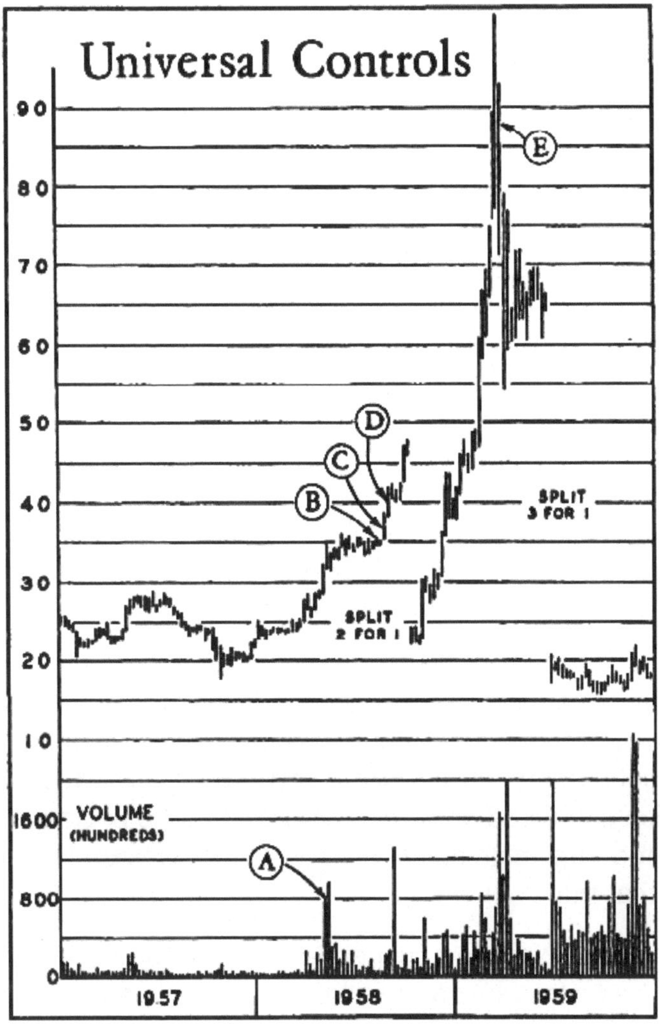

THIOKOL CHEMICAL

In Tokyo early in 1958, Darvas noticed sudden heavy trading in this stock following a 2-for-l split (A). It remained quiet for some months afterwards, but to Darvas this "tranquility" had the feeling of "a calm that precedes the storm".

Soon after Darvas started getting daily quotes, THIOKOL "looked as though it was flexing its muscles for an upward jump" from 45, and he made a pilot buy of 200 shares at 47¼ (B). For four weeks the stock kept pushing toward 50, and at (C), just as Darvas felt it was ready to break through, he bought 1,300 shares at 49⅞-

On the heels of this purchase came THIOKOL'S issuance of stock rights. In an inspired series of transactions, which are fully explained in the text, Darvas took maximum advantage of the tremendous credit that is available when rights are exercised. Through the purchase of 72,000 rights (and the sale of his first 1,500 shares at 53½), he acquired 6,000 shares of THIOKOL stock at the subscription price of $42 per share (when the quoted price was in the middle 50's). His cash outlay was only $111,000 towards the total purchase price of $3 50,000.

Three months later (D) his broker wired him that he had a profit of $250,000 on his THIOKOL investment. As he walked, tormented with temptation, through the streets of Paris, "every fiber in my being seemed to be saying ‘sell, sell’ "—but he held on to the stock.

Of course, Darvas never for a moment forgot to move his stop-loss up as the stock rose, but with THIOKOL he allowed a greater leeway of movement so as not to risk being stopped out on a short-lived reaction such as did occur at (E). The rise which followed, and which continued after the 3-for-l split at the beginning of May, culminated in a high-point of 72 accompanied by such hectic trading that the

N. Y. Stock Exchange suspended the use of all automatic on-stop and stop-loss buy and sell orders for this stock. For Darvas this meant "they had taken my most powerful tool away, and I could not work without it".

He sold his 18,000 split shares at an average price of 68 (F), for a total profit of 862,000. The momentous decision in Paris - "You have no reason to sell a rising stock" - had paid off.

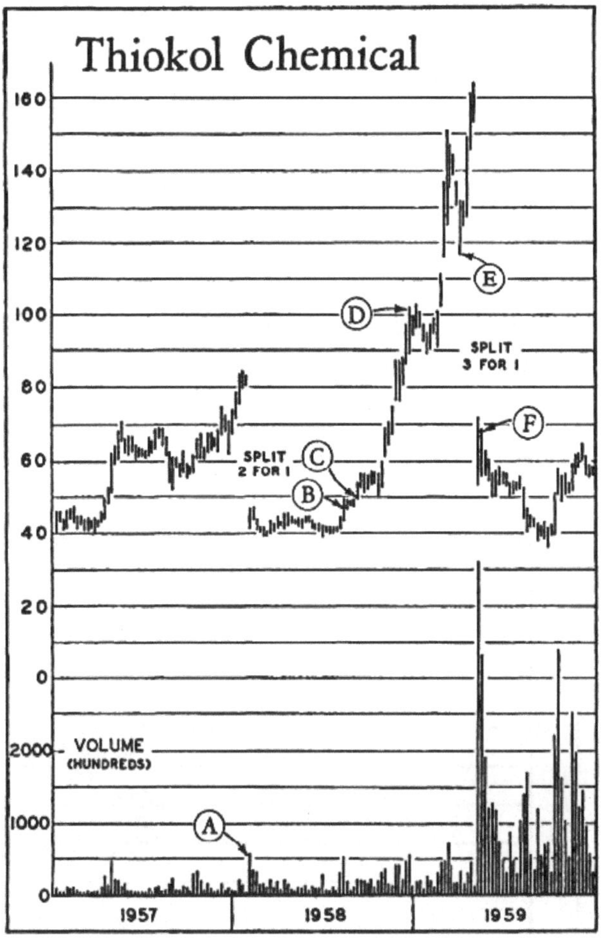

TEXAS INSTRUMENTS

After his sale of UNIVERSAL CONTROLS, Darvas "took a careful look at the market . . . for an actively traded, high-priced stock" in which to invest over a half-million dollars. With such a large sum involved, he had also to allow for the possibility that his buying might affect the market.

Except for some slightly erratic behavior at the end of 1958, TEXAS INSTRUMENTS had been moving steadily upward for over a year, and the velocity of its advance had increased coincidentally with a marked rise in volume (A) in October.

Darvas bought 2,000 shares the second week in April (B) at an average price of 94⅜. The following week, "as the stock continued to act well", he acquired 1,500 more at 97⅞ (C). Within a few days he made a final purchase of 2,000 shares at an average of 101⅞ (D) •

On July 6th, TEXAS INSTRUMENTS closed at 149½ (E), and it is at this point that Darvas takes off for Monte Carlo at the end of Chapter 10, with a new set of adjusted stop-losses waiting somewhere below the closing prices of his more than $2,250,000 worth of holdings.

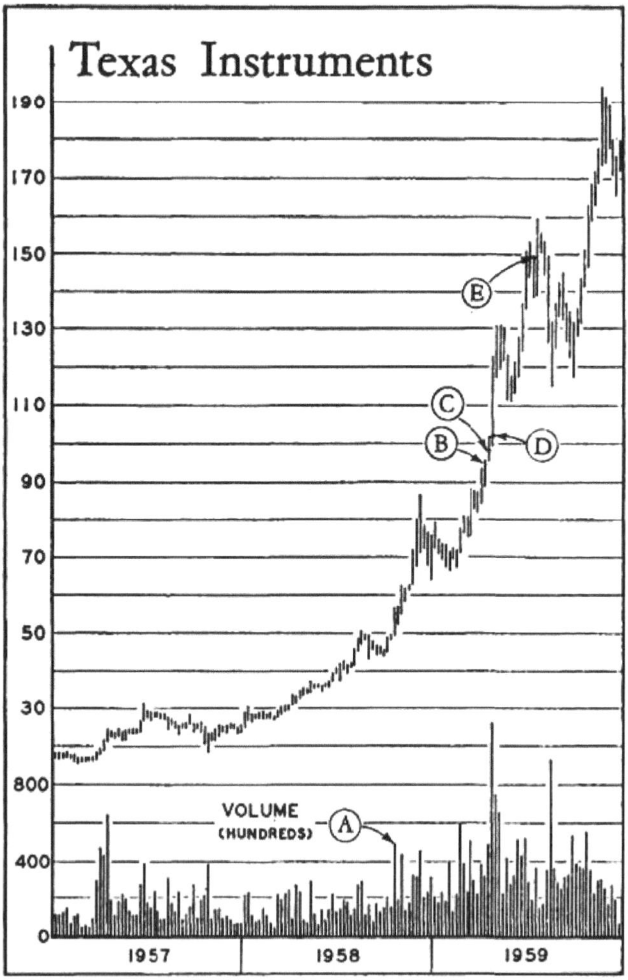

FAIRCHILD CAMERA

The sale of THIOKOL left Darvas with an investment capital of over $1,000,000. Having decided to divide this into two parts, he narrowed his choice to four stocks, which he had been watching for a long time and which were "all suitable as far as my techno-fundamentalist theory was concerned".

One of the stocks that survived a test buy to determine the relative market strength of the four was FAIRCHILD CAMERA.

FAIRCHILD had been very stable in price throughout 1957 and most of 1958 despite two periods of tremendous increases in trading volume. But at the end of 1958 a new jump in volume (A) was complemented by a rapid and almost continuous rise in the price of the stock, at which point it became interesting to Darvas.

He made his pilot buy of 500 shares at 128 (B), when the stock had established itself in a 110/140 box. Having removed the arbitrary 10% stop-loss, which was too close with respect to the lower limit of the box, he was unaffected by the low of 110¼ which occurred two weeks later. On the contrary, as the stock re-established its upward momentum almost immediately, he bought 4,000 additional shares at (C) for prices ranging from 123¼ to 127.

With his holdings of 4,500 shares of FAIRCHILD CAMERA along with ZENITH RADIO and TEXAS INSTRUMENTS, Darvas was now in a position to sit "on the sidelines just keeping vigil while my stocks continued to climb steadily like well-made missiles". As of the end of this book, FAIRCHILD CAMERA closed at 185 (D).

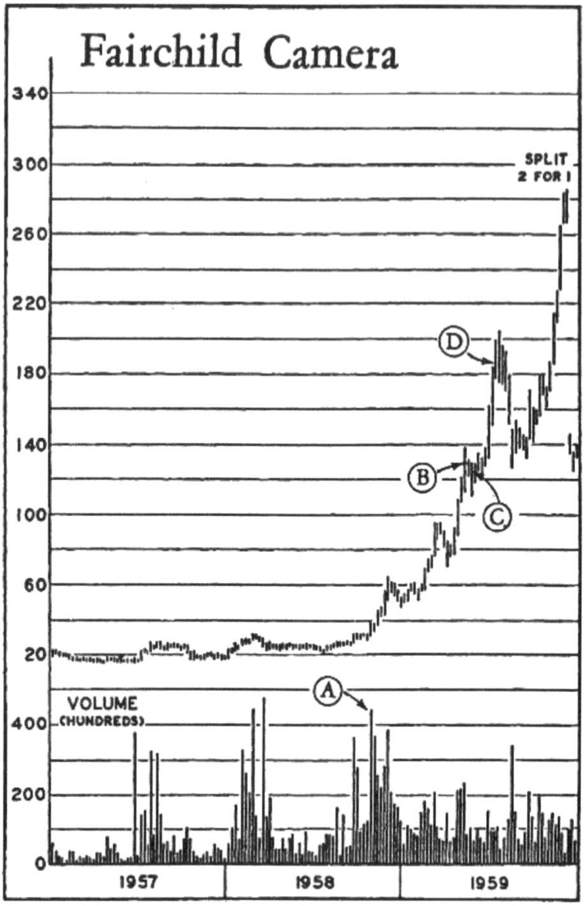

ZENITH RADIO

This is the second of the stocks into which Darvas switched the capital that THIOKOL had built for him, and it is quite different from FAIRCHILD in its pattern prior to the time of this investment. Peak trading in ZENITH at the end of September 1958 was accompanied by an explosive price advance for this already volatile stock.

Darvas made his pilot buy at 104 (A) on a "when-issued" basis just after announcement of a 3-for-l split. As with FAIRCHILD, he dropped the arbitrary 10% stop-loss, which he had set up to eliminate the weakest of the four stocks, he was interested in. Had he kept it there, he would have been sold out the following week when ZENITH dropped to 93. However, as the price immediately started an upward move, he proceeded as planned and bought 5,000 shares at prices ranging from 99¾ to 107½ (B).

ZENITH moved along nicely after that, and it is worth noting that though its progress was unspectacular compared to its pre-split rise, the "little" difference between his average buy price of 104 and the closing price of 124 (C) on July 6th, when the book ends, represented a profit for Darvas of more than $ 100,000.

When they were writing up these charts, our editors pointed out to Darvas that his purchase of ZENITH so late in its rise looked anticlimactic. He agreed and said, "By hindsight it seems to have been late in its rise—at the time it looked to me like the beginning of a new rise. After all, I only expect to be right half the time."

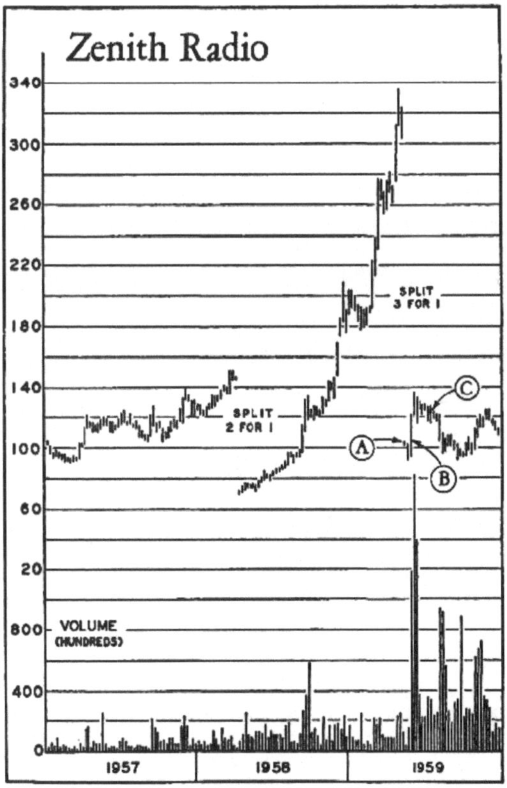

LIST OF TITLES WITH ISBN NO.

ISBN	TITLE
9788194914129	1984
9789390575220	1984 & Animal Farm (2In1)
9789390575572	1984 & Animal Farm (2In1): The International Best-Selling Classics
9789390575848	35 Sonnets
9789390575329	A Clergyman's Daughter
9789390575923	A Study In Scarlet
9789390896097	A Tale Of Two Cities
9789390896837	Abide in Christ
9789390896202	Abraham Lincoln
9789390896912	Absolute Surrender
9789390896608	African American Classic Collection
9789390575305	Aldous Huxley: The Collected Works
9789390896141	An Autobiography of M. K. Gandhi
9789390575886	Animal Farm
9789390575619	Animal Farm & The Great Gatsby (2In1)
9789390575626	Animal Farm & We
9789390896158	Anna Karenina
9789390575534	Antic Hay
9789390896165	Antony & Cleopatra
9789390896172	As I Lay Dying
9789390896226	As You like it
9789390575671	At Your Command
9789390575350	Awakened Imagination
9789390575114	Be What You Wish
9789390896233	Believe In yourself
9789390896998	Best of Charles Darwin: The Origin of Species & Autobiography
9789390896684	Best Of Horror : Dracula And Frankenstein
9789390575503	Best Of Mark Twain (The Adventures of Tom Sawyer AND The Adventures of Huckleberry Finn)
9789390896769	Black History Collection
9789390575756	Brave New World, Animal Farm & 1984 (3in1)

9789390896240	Brother Karamzov
9789390575053	Bulleh Shah Poetry
9789390575725	Burmese Days
9789390896257	Bushido
9789390896066	Can't Hurt Me
9788194914112	Chanakya Neeti: With The Complete Sutras
9789390896042	Crime and Punishment
9789390575527	Crome Yellow
9789390575046	Down and Out in Paris and London
9789390896844	Dracula
9789390575442	Emersons Essays: The Complete First & Second Series (Self-Reliance & Other Essays)
9789390575749	Emma
9789390575817	Essential Tozer Collection - The Pursuit of God & The Purpose of Man
9789390896578	Fascism What It Is and How to Fight It
9789390575688	Feeling is the Secret
9789390575190	Five Lessons
9789390575954	Frankenstein
9789390575237	Franz Kafka: Collected Works
9789390575282	Franz Kafka: Short Stories
9789390575060	George Orwell Collected Works
9789390575077	George Orwell Essays
9789390575213	George Orwell Poems
9788194914150	Greatest Poetry Ever Written Vol 1
9788194914143	Greatest Poetry Ever Written Vol 1
9789390896301	Gulliver's Travel
9789390575961	Gunaho Ka Devta
9789390575893	H. P. Lovecraft Selected Stories Vol 1
9789390575978	H. P. Lovecraft Selected Stories Vol 2
9789390896059	Hamlet
9789390575022	His Last Bow: Some Reminiscences of Sherlock Holmes
9789390896134	History of Western Philosophy
9789390575121	Homage To Catalonia

9789390896219	How to develop self-confidence and Improve public Speaking
9789390896295	How to enjoy your life and your Job
9789390575633	How to own your own mind
9789390896318	How to read Human Nature
9789390896325	How to sell your way through the life
9789390896370	How to use the laws of mind
9789390896387	How to use the power of prayer
9789390896028	How to win friends & Influence People
9788194824176	How To Win Friends and Influence People
9789390896103	Humility The Beauty of Holiness
9789390896653	Imperialism the Highest Stage of Capitalism
9789390575084	In Our Time
9789390575169	In Our Time & Three Stories and Ten poems
9789390575145	James Allen: The Collected Works
9789390896189	Jesus Himself
9789390575480	Jo's Boys
9789390896394	Julius Caesar
9789390575404	Keep the Aspidistra Flying
9789390896400	Kidnapped
9789390896424	King Lear
9789390575824	Lady Susan
9789390896455	Law of Success
9789390896264	Lincoln The Unknown
9789390575565	Little Men
9789390575640	Little Women
9788194914174	Lost Horizon
9789390896462	Macbeth
9789390896929	Man Eaters of Kumaon
9789390896523	Man The Dwelling Place of God
9789390896349	Man The Dwelling Place of God
9789390575909	Mansfield Park
9788194914136	Manto Ki 25 Sarvshreshth Kahaniya
9789390896509	Marxism, Anarchism, Communism
9789390575664	Mathematical Principles of Natural Philosophy

9788194914198	Meditations
9789390575800	Mein Kampf
9789390575794	Memory How To Develop, Train, And Use It
9789390896486	Mind Power
9789390896585	Money
9789390575039	Mortal Coils
9789390575770	My Life and Work
9789390896035	Narrative of the Life of Frederick Douglass
9789390575152	Neville Goddard: The Collected Works
9789390575985	Northanger Abbey
9789390896530	Notes From Underground
9789390896547	Oliver Twist
9789390575459	On War
9789390575541	One, None and a Hundred Thousand
9789390896554	Othelo
9789390575435	Out Of This World
9789390575015	Persuasion
9789390575510	Prayer The Art Of Believing
9789390575091	Pride and Prejudice
9789390896561	Psychic Perception
9789390575381	Rabindranath Tagore - 5 Best Short Stories Vol 2
9789390575367	Rabindranath Tagore - Short Stories (Masters Collections Including The Childs Return)
9789390575374	Rabindranath Tagore 5 Best Short Stories Vol 1 (Including The Childs Return
9789390896622	Romeo & Juliet
9789390896127	Sanatana Dharma
9789390575596	Seedtime & Harvest
9789390896639	Selected Stories of Guy De Maupassant
9789390575206	Self-Reliance & Other Essays
9789390575176	Sense and Sensibility
9789390575299	Shyamchi Aai
9789390896738	Socialism Utopian and Scientific
9789390896646	Success Through a Positive Mental Attitude
9789390575428	The Adventures of Huckleberry Finn

9789390575183	The Adventures of Sherlock Holmes
9789390575343	The Adventures of Tom Sawyer
9789390896691	The Alchemy Of Happiness
9789390575862	The Art Of Public Speaking
9789390896288	The Autobiography Of Charles Darwin
9788194914181	The Best of Franz Kafka: The Metamorphosis & The Trial
9789390575008	The Call Of Cthulhu and Other Weird Tales
9789390575107	The Case-Book of Sherlock Holmes
9789390896110	The Castle Of Otranto
9789390896745	The Communist Manifesto
9789390575589	The Complete Fiction of H. P. Lovecraft
9789390575497	The Complete Works of Florence Scovel Shinn
9789390896820	The Conquest of Breard
9789390896813	The Diary of a Young Girl
9789390896332	The Diary of a Young Girl The Definitive Edition of the Worlds Most Famous Diary
9789390575701	The Great Gatsby, Animal Farm & 1984 (3In1)
9789390575312	The Greatest Works Of George Orwell (5 Books) Including 1984 & Non-Fiction
9789390575992	The Hound of Baskervilles
9789390896707	The Idiot
9789390896714	The Invisible Man
9789390575657	The Knowledge of the holy
9789390575558	The Law & the Promise
9789390896721	The Law Of Attraction
9789390896776	The Leader in you
9789390896363	The Life of Christ
9789390896196	The Man-Eating Leopard of Rudraprayag
9789390896783	The Master Key to Riches
9789390575268	The Memoirs Of Sherlock Holmes
9789390896479	The Midsummer Night's Dream
9789390575466	The Mill On The Floss
9789390896790	The Miracles of your mind
9789390896660	The Mutual Aid A Factor in Evolution
9789390896448	The Origin of Species

9789390896905	The Peter Kropotkin Anthology The Conquest of Bread & Mutual Aid A Factor of Evolution
9789390896806	The Picture of Dorian Gray
9789390896271	The Picture of Dorian Gray
9789390575275	The Power Of Awareness
9789390896356	The Power of Concentration
9788194824169	The Power of Positive Thinking
9789390575411	The Power of the Spoken Word
9788194914105	The Power Of Your Subconscious Mind
9789390896899	The Power of Your Subconscious Mind
9789390896417	The Principles of Communism
9789390575787	The Psychology Of Mans Possible Evolution
9789390896615	The Psychology of Salesmanship
9789390575732	The Pursuit of God
9789390575398	The Pursuit of Happiness
9789390896851	The Quick and Easy Way to effective Speaking
9789390575947	The Return Of Sherlock Holmes
9789390575138	The Road To Wigan Pier
9789390896981	The Root of the Righteous
9789390575855	The Science Of Being Well
9788194914167	The Science Of Getting Rich, The Science Of Being Great & The Science Of Being Well (3In1)
9789390896011	The Screwtape Letters
9789390896073	The Screwtape Letters
9789390575336	The Secret Door to Success
9789390575695	The Secret Of Imagining
9789390896868	The Secret Of Success
9789390896431	The Seven Last Words
9789390575930	The Sign of the Four
9789390896004	The Sonnets
9789390896516	The Souls of Black Folk
9789390896875	The Sound and The Fury
9789390575244	The State and Revolution
9789390896882	The Story of My Life
9789390896936	The Story Of Oriental Philosophy

9789390896752	The Strange Case of Dr. Jekyll and Mr. Hyde
9789390896943	The Tempest
9789390575916	The Valley Of Fear
9789390575879	The Wind in the willows
9789390896080	The Wind in the willows
9789390575763	Their eyes were watching gofd
9789390575831	Three Stories
9789390896950	Twelfth Night
9789390896592	Twelve Years a Slave
9789390896677	Up from Slavery
9789390896974	Value Price and Profit
9789390896967	Wake Up and Live
9789390896493	With Christ in the School of Prayer
9789390575602	Your Faith is Your Fortune
9789390575473	Your Infinite Power To Be Rich
9789390575251	Your Word is Your Wand
9789390575718	Youth
9789391316099	A Christmas Carol
9789391316105	A Doll's House
9789391316501	A Passage to India
9789391316709	A Portrait of the Artist as a Young Man
9789391316112	A Tale of Two Cities
9789391316747	A Tear and a Smile
9789391316167	Agnes Gray
9789391316174	Alice's Adventures in Wonderland
9789391316136	Anandamath
9789391316181	Anne Of Green Gables
9789391316754	Anthem
9789391316198	Around The World in 80 Days
9789391316013	As A Man Thinketh
9789391316242	Autobiography of a Yogi
9789391316266	Beyond Good and Evil
9789391316761	Bleak House
9789391316778	Chitra, a Play in One Act
9789391316310	David Copperfield

9789391316075	Demian
9789391316785	Dubliners
9789391316051	Favourite Tales from the Arabian Nights
9789391316235	Gitanjali
9789391316068	Gravity
9789391316150	Great Speeches of Abraham Lincoln
9789391316662	Guerilla Warfare
9789391316839	Kim
9789391316822	Mother
9789391316211	My Childhood
9789391316846	Nationalism
9789391316327	Oliver Twist
9789391316853	Pygmalion
9789391316334	Relativity: The Special and the General Theory
9789391316389	Scientific Healing Affirmation
9789391316341	Sons and Lovers
9789391316587	Tales from India
9789391316372	Tess of The D'Urbervilles
9789391316396	The Awakening and Selected Stories
9789391316402	The Bhagvad Gita
9789391316303	The Book of Enoch
9789391316228	The Canterville Ghost
9789391316907	The Dynamic Laws of Prosperity
9789391316006	The Great Gatsby
9789391316860	The Hungry Stones and Other Stories
9789391316433	The Idiot
9789391316440	The Importance of Being Earnest
9789391316297	The Light of Asia
9789391316914	The Madman His Parables and Poems
9789391316457	The Odyssey
9789391316921	The Picture of Dorian Gray
9789391316464	The Prince
9789391316938	The Prophet
9789391316945	The Republic
9789391316518	The Scarlet Letter

9789391316143	The Seven Laws of Teaching
9789391316525	The Story of My Experiments with Truth
9789391316532	The Tales of the Mother Goose
9789391316549	The Thirty Nine Steps
9789391316594	The Time Machine
9789391316600	The Turn of the Screw
9789391316983	The Upanishads
9789391316617	The Yellow Wallpaper
9789391316426	The Yoga Sutras of Patanjali
9789391316990	Ulysses
9789391316624	Utopia
9789391316679	Vanity Fair
9789391316020	What Is To Be Done
9789391316686	Within A Budding Grove
9789391316693	Women in Love